THE
YARN GARDEN

30+ knits using plant-based fibers

kp
KRAUSE PUBLICATIONS
CINCINNATI, OHIO

mycraftivity.com
connect. create. explore.

J. MARSHA MICHLER

The Yarn Garden: 30+ Knits Using Plant-Based Fibers. Copyright ©
2009 by J. Marsha Michler. Manufactured in China. All rights reserved. The
patterns and drawings in this book are for the personal use of the reader.
By permission of the author and publisher, they may be either hand-
traced or photocopied to make single copies, but under no circumstances
may they be resold or republished. No other part of this book may be
reproduced in any form or by any electronic or mechanical means including
information storage and retrieval systems without permission in writing
from the publisher, except by a reviewer who may quote brief passages in a
review. Author and Publisher are not liable for any damages occurring due
to errors in the instructions. Published by Krause Publications, an imprint of
F+W Media, Inc., 4700 East Galbraith Road, Cincinnati, Ohio, 45236. (800)
289-0963. First Edition.

www.fwmedia.com.

13 12 11 10 09   5 4 3 2 1

DISTRIBUTED IN CANADA BY FRASER DIRECT
100 Armstrong Avenue
Georgetown, ON, Canada L7G 5S4
Tel: (905) 877-4411

DISTRIBUTED IN THE U.K. AND EUROPE BY DAVID & CHARLES
Brunel House, Newton Abbot, Devon, TQ12 4PU, England
Tel: (+44) 1626 323200, Fax: (+44) 1626 323319
Email: postmaster@davidandcharles.co.uk

DISTRIBUTED IN AUSTRALIA BY CAPRICORN LINK
P.O. Box 704, S. Windsor NSW, 2756 Australia
Tel: (02) 4577-3555

Library of Congress Cataloging in Publication Data
Michler, J. Marsha.
  The yarn garden : 30+ knits using plant-based fibers / J. Marsha Michler.
     p. cm.
  Includes index.
  ISBN 978-0-89689-827-1 (alk. paper)
  1. Knitting--Patterns. 2. Crocheting--Patterns. 3. Sweaters. 4. Plant fibers.
  I. Title.
  TT825.M5425 2009
  746.43'2--dc22
                        2009018319

Editor: Jennifer Claydon
Designer: Michelle Thompson
Production coordinator: Matt Wagner
Photographer: Ric Deliantoni
Technical Editor: Amy Polcyn
Stylist: Megan Strasser
Makeup Artist: Cass Brake
Illustrator: Hayes Shanesy (select illustrations only)

*F+W Media would like to thank the following for generously
sharing the beautiful locations shown in this book:
Baker Hunt Art and Cultural Center, Kate Cook & Dave Schwinn,
Steve Paszt, Susan Pelle & Melissa Spencer, Cathy & Ric Strasser.*

METRIC CONVERSION CHART

To convert	to	multiply by
Inches	Centimeters	2.54
Centimeters	Inches	0.4
Feet	Centimeters	30.5
Centimeters	Feet	0.03
Yards	Meters	0.9
Meters	Yards	1.1
Ounces	Grams	28.3
Grams	Ounces	0.035

ABOUT THE AUTHOR

J. Marsha Michler is the author of twelve books about crazy
quilting, jewelry and knitting. She has written many articles
for magazines and has won quilt awards for her crazy quilts.
She actively pursues various needlearts, jewelry-making,
spinning, pottery, photography and Web site design. In her
spare time she gardens, builds stone walls, travels and enjoys
sushi with her husband. She resides in the beautiful foothills
of Southern Maine. To learn more about Marsha, visit her
Web site: http://www.jmarshamichler.com.

ACKNOWLEDGMENTS

A great many thanks to Candy Wiza for both suggesting this book idea and getting me the job. I appreciate your efforts and I have to say, it has been a wonderful adventure!

Many, many thanks to those who answered my questions, sent samples and contributed luxurious, gorgeous skeins of knitting stuffs to this endeavor. They are Donna Yacino at Berroco Inc., Sylvia Hager at Blue Sky Alpacas, Shannon at Cascade Yarns, Stephanie at Frabjous Fibers, Stephanie at Ecobutterfly, Lena at Garnstudio, Halcyon Blake at Halcyon Yarn, Anni Kristensen at Himalaya Yarn, Jana Dempsey at Hand Maiden Fine Yarn, Lana Hames at Lanaknits Designs, Kim Cameron at Knit Picks, Susan Moraca at Kollage Yarns,

John Hartley at Louet North America, Joyce Rodriguez at Knit One, Crochet Too, Inc., Jonelle Raffino at South West Trading Company, Deborah Errico at Tahki Stacy Charles, Inc. and Linda Pratt at Westminster Fibers. Without your support this would have been a very different book.

Thanks as well to my ever-patient editor, Jenni Claydon—you are a pleasure to work with! And thanks to designer, Michelle Thompson and photographer, Ric Deliantoni.

And a very special thanks to my husband, Gil, for all of the gourmet dinners and for patiently wading through piles of yarns and half-knitted sweaters. You are the perfect partner.

CONTENTS

INTRODUCTION

After using wool yarns for the majority of my knitting life, it has been a horizon-expanding and rewarding experience to explore plant-based yarns. Until recently, the number of plant-based yarns available to knitters was limited. However, there is now a garden's worth of variety in these yarns. The recent rise in interest in both knitting and sustainability has caused a corresponding rise in the number of plant-based yarns available. Traditional favorites like cotton and linen have been given new life, and lesser-known fibers like nettle and hemp are being introduced to knitters as new options.

One category of plant-based fibers, extruded fibers, have been manufactured for many years, but are new to most knitters. These fibers are manufactured from plant fibers such as wood, soy, corn and bamboo. Rayon, the first extruded fiber, was created to imitate silk. The different yarns in this group vary in terms of texture and finish. Exploring these new and exciting fibers will open many design avenues for knitters, and I will introduce you to all of them in the following pages.

Plant-based yarns are available in a wide variety of finishes, ranging from matte to lustrous and from smooth to coarse. You can use them to create fabrics that are snug and soft, crisp and smooth or elegant and flowing. As an added bonus, all are a pleasure to knit with and feel wonderful next to the skin—there isn't an itchy one in the bunch. Most plant-based yarns are cool in hot weather, which means they are pleasant to knit with in the warmer months, extending the knitting season from winter only to year-round. This also means your wardrobe can include handknits for any season.

Join me on an exploration of these incredible yarns. I recommend starting with small sample skeins of plant-based yarns; examine the yarns, knit or crochet swatches, then take them through the washing process, and get to know them. After sampling, pick your favorites and use them to make garments you will love. Immerse yourself in a yarn garden for all seasons!

MATERIALS AND TOOLS

Now is an exciting time to be a knitter. We have a wider range of fibers to knit with than ever before. Wool and other animal fibers are superb natural fibers and knitters will always love working with them, but I, for one, am delighted with plant-based yarns as well. They extend both the knitting season and the sweater-wearing season. Most plant-based yarns are comfortable to knit with even in warm weather, and many feel cool to wear in summer's heat. These yarns offer textures and finishes that stand apart from wool, creating unique looks for your wardrobe.

The notable differences between wools and plant-based fibers are weight, drape and texture. Plant-based fibers tend to weigh more than wool, and weights vary among the different fibers. Garments made from plant-based yarns will weigh a bit more than those made from animal-based yarns. Drape is also different in plant-based fibers, especially linen, hemp and extruded fibers. These fibers create graceful and elegant fabrics that both flow and mold themselves to the body. Most of the fibers tend to be smooth, soft and sometimes silky, unlike wool. Plant-based yarns are wonderful options for those who don't care to wear wool, or who have allergies to it.

The yarn creation methods for plant-based yarns vary widely in eco-friendliness. But overall, raising plants takes up less space than farming for production of animal fibers, prevents erosion and does not require large amounts of feed. And fair-trade practices are a part of some of the fibers produced in different parts of the world.

No special tools are needed for knitting and crocheting plant-based fibers. You can use the knitting tools you already have to explore the world of plant-based yarns.

PLANT-BASED YARNS

Plant-based yarns are almost always manufactured in one of two ways. They are either made of strands of fiber spun and plied into yarn, or they are knitted tubes made of one fine strand of fiber. The knitted tubes are called ribbon yarns. Ribbon yarns are just as easy to knit with as the plied yarns, and they can be made from soy, bamboo, corn, cotton and other fibers.

I've also found that plant-based yarns can be placed into three distinct categories based on the type of fiber used to create the yarn (a fourth category, recycled yarns, is not unique to a certain type of fiber). These are bast fibers, cotton and extruded fibers. Each of these categories, and each of the yarns in each category, has its own unique features. Weight, texture and structure are all varied, and all take a part in the final garment—give these features the attention they deserve and you will be rewarded with beautiful knits.

BAST FIBERS

Bast fibers are the food-conducting tissues found in the long, woody stems of many plants. These fibers can be processed through either natural or chemical means. Bast fiber yarns are coarse until they have been washed, and sometimes require several washings to soften them. They often feel stringy in knitting, and can be knitted in the coarse stage, or washed first to soften them. Fabrics made of bast fibers take well to ironing, gaining a subtle sheen from it—they often have a soft luster to begin with. An additional benefit is that bast fibers are very long wearing. Among bast fiber yarns there is a range of weights (yarn thicknesses); subtle characteristics of spinning, especially in artisan yarns; and a wide range of gorgeous dyed and natural colors.

HEMP

Hemp has been used for thousands of years to make rope, clothing and footwear. In the U.S. there has been controversy over the industrial hemp plant's close resemblance to an illegal drug plant, but the two are not the same. Industrial hemp can be legally grown in the U.S. but this is discouraged through heavy regulations. Industrial hemp is an environmentally friendly crop. The plant attracts few pests and grows so closely that weeds cannot compete. Because it grows closely, with a high ratio of stalk growth to leaf growth, it is a productive crop.

The fibers used to make hemp yarns are taken from the stalks of the plant, which are quite long—typically 3'–15' (1m–5m). The stalks are harvested and dried and then the fibers are separated from the core of the stalk through a process called retting. The resulting fibers have a long staple, or length, averaging 8" (20cm). Depending on the type of processing used, the natural color of hemp can be creamy white, brown, gray, black or green.

HEMP CHARACTERISTICS

Hemp is a strong and durable fiber either wet or dry. It is very absorbent, cool and comfortable to wear, resistant to mildew and antimicrobial. Hemp blocks UV rays better than any other fiber. Keeping its shape through many wearings, it can be machine washed and dried, it doesn't pill and it dyes well. Hemp yarns can feel coarse before knitting, but will soften upon washing and wearing.

LINEN

Linen yarns are created from the bast fibers of the flax plant. Linen is thought to be the first plant fiber to be made into cloth. The earliest recorded established linen industry was in Egypt 4,000 years ago. The British Museum in London has pieces of linen in its collection that are 6,000 years old. Linen fibers have survived the test of time where other fibers have long decomposed.

The stalk of the flax plant is typically 3½'–4' (1m) tall. To make linen, the flax is harvested, then dried or placed into retting ponds. The flax is then retted by chemical or natural processes. Retting is followed by scutching, which is the process of crushing the stalks to remove the woody part of the stalk. The long flax fibers are then removed and either spun, bleached or dyed.

LINEN CHARACTERISTICS

Linen is 2 to 3 times stronger than cotton. The fabric is lustrous and lint-free, stands up to heat, and gets softer with washings. It is highly absorbent and cool to wear. Elasticity is poor, and it tends to crack along crease lines.

NETTLE

This bast fiber is a product of the Himalayan giant nettle. Grown at high elevations in the Himalayas, it reaches heights of 12'–16' (4m–5m). The fibers are processed by hand in a method similar to the retting of linen. Nettle is a strong, somewhat rough fiber that is traditionally used for fishing nets and totes. Additional processing softens the fibers enough for garment production. Despite this, nettle yarns can still feel a little coarse during knitting, but the knitted fabric feels soft after washing.

NETTLE CHARACTERISTICS

Nettle fibers are moth and bug repellent and commonly used along with wool by carpet manufacturers. It also irons well on a wool setting. The natural shades of the fiber create soft stripes in the knitting.

COTTON

Cotton is unique among plant-based fibers; no other fiber or yarn is produced from a seedpod as cotton is. And it is the only one presented here that you can grow yourself (given a suitable climate), pick, spin and knit. One might think of cotton as being pretty ordinary and mundane, but very exciting things are happening with cotton these days. Cotton is now being grown in a beautiful variety of colors and for these no dyes are needed. Cotton yarns range from coarse to soft, with finer, thread-like cottons at one end of the scale and soft, fluffy yarns at the other. Some cotton yarns are wound with a finer strand to give them better shape retention. Softness is their overriding characteristic by far, and most finishes are matte. Another benefit of cotton is its comfort appeal—there is nothing as nice as a cotton sweater worn to near-shapelessness

The cotton plant is a tropical and subtropical shrub that produces a fluffy boll around its seeds. Cotton has long been used to make clothing, with the earliest recorded pieces dating to about 3000 B.C. in India and South America. Cotton is still the most commonly used clothing fiber. Industrial cotton growing requires irrigation, pesticides, herbicides and genetic engineering.

ORGANIC COTTON

Organic cotton is grown in a much more eco-friendly way than industrial cotton, and the fibers undergo much less processing than mercerized cottons. It is grown without pesticides and insecticides and processed without chemicals or dye (dyes are chemicals and many are environmentally damaging—some countries have banned certain dyes because they are so harmful).

Many organic cottons are available in gorgeous natural colors such as cream, beige, brown, avocado and mauve, as you can see in the *Mountain Flora* sweater on page 26. These colors sometimes darken upon washing in hot water. Because the color is inherent, it does not fade. Although they are new to many of us, colored cottons are not a new invention. Colored cottons have always occurred naturally, although almost all were destroyed when industry demanded white cottons. However, many people still grew them and quantities continue to increase. Some of these yarns are Fair Trade Certified, meaning the workers who grow the cotton and produce the yarn are provided with fair wages and good living conditions.

The University of Agricultural Sciences in India is conducting research on growing cotton organically and creating colored cottons genetically. Some chemical dyes have been banned in India, among other countries, making naturally colored cotton an attractive idea.

MERCERIZED COTTON

Mercerized cotton yarns are made from cotton fibers that have been through several chemical processes. First, a bath in an alkali solution rounds and straightens the cotton fibers. This process also helps the fibers absorb dye more readily. Next, the fibers are put under tension, which prevents them from shrinking, and also causes them to gain luster. Mercerized cotton is also known as pearl or perle cotton. Mercerized yarns are preshrunk and stronger than unmercerized yarns.

COTTON CHARACTERISTICS
Cotton is comfortable, soft, absorbent, withstands high temperatures, stands up to abrasion, wears well, and is a strong fiber both wet and dry. It is machine washable and dry cleanable.

EXTRUDED FIBERS

Extruded fibers are made of plant material that is liquefied, then extruded through a spinnerette and finally solidified to create fine fibers. Yarns created from extruded fibers are available in a range of weights and colors. Each of these yarns has unique characteristics, but all drape beautifully—so much so that some of them tend to relax after knitting and washing, growing slightly, as opposed to shrinking. Some are created to have a high gloss, and these yarns can be slippery and difficult to knit with. Quite often extruded fibers are blended with cotton, adding drape, sheen and a silky feel to the characteristics of cotton.

LYOCELL

Lyocell is a manufactured cellulose fiber made from wood pulp. The wood pulp is dissolved using a solvent, then returned to fiber form, spun, washed, finished and dried. The manufacturing process uses no bleach and the solvent is eco-friendly, biodegradable, and nearly 100 percent reclaimed. The European Union awarded this process the European Business Award for the Environment 2000 in the category "technology for sustainable developments." Lyocell is a generic term for this type of fiber and Tencel is a common trade name.

First introduced to consumers in 1991, it was categorized by the Federal Trade Commission as a subvariety of rayon that is made using an organic solvent spinning process.

LYOCELL CHARACTERISTICS

Lyocell has a fluid, silky drape and is lustrous like silk. Much like cotton, it is breathable, absorbent and wicks away moisture. It accepts dyes easily, resists wrinkling and shrinkage, and is strong when wet or dry. It is washable by machine or hand, and dry cleanable.

SEAWEED

There is no yarn that is derived entirely from seaweed, but there is a new fiber on the market called Seacell, which is composed of Lyocell (see above) with a small amount of seaweed added (approximately 5 percent). Lyocell is used as a "carrier" for the seaweed, which imparts qualities previously available only in cosmetics into clothing. Seaweed is rich in minerals, trace elements, fats and carbohydrates. Tests conducted in Germany found that the active elements in seaweed are released when in contact with the natural humidity of human skin.

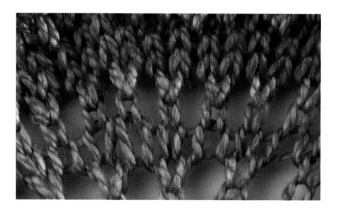

SEAWEED CHARACTERISTICS

The characteristics of Lyocell apply to this yarn.

BAMBOO

Bamboo is a grass, and also an evergreen woody perennial known to be the fastest growing plant on earth. There are a thousand species of bamboo. The plant is not killed by harvesting, because new shoots continually emerge from its root system.

Bamboo yarns are made using two methods. Fiber can be taken straight from the plant and then processed by steaming, decomposing and degumming before it is carded. Or, it can be made from bamboo pulp, similar to rayon and Lyocell. This process is environmentally friendly, does not use chemical additives, and the resulting fiber composts naturally. The fibers created in this manner are finer than a strand of hair.

In a cross section of bamboo fiber, small holes and gaps are evident. These allow a fabric made of bamboo to be absorbent and breathable.

BAMBOO CHARACTERISTICS

Bamboo is a very wearable fiber. Due to its absorbency it requires less dye, and can be dyed with natural dyes. As a fabric it drapes with elegance, feels silky and soft, and is cool to wear in hot weather. It is antimicrobial, resistant to UV rays, and odor-resistant. Similar to rayon, in water it swells and loses strength.

CORN

Corn fiber is a synthetic made from animal-feed corn. The resulting fiber is similar to polyester. The process used to make corn fiber takes natural sugar from the corn and ferments it, then melts and extrudes it into a fine thread which is then spun and processed into yarn for textiles.

The process is more eco-friendly than deriving polyester fiber from petroleum because foreign oil is not used in the product itself, and 20–50 percent less fossil fuels are required in the fiber's production. However, corn fiber is twice as expensive to produce as polyester. Unlike polyester, corn fiber decomposes naturally.

CORN CHARACTERISTICS

Corn yarns are lighter than bamboo. The fabric has a beautiful drape and is appropriate for wear in any season. It can be machine washed and dried. Corn yarn cannot be ironed, because it will melt. The fiber is strong and soft, and known for its wicking ability.

MODAL

Modal is a variety of rayon (see below) which is made from the cellulose of beech trees. The process of making Modal fiber involves heavy processing and chemicals, and so it is referred to as "bio-based" rather than natural. Modal is used in household linens and clothing.

MODAL CHARACTERISTICS

Modal fiber is soft, smoother than mercerized cotton, and can be mercerized like cotton. It is more stable than rayon when wet, and is strong and wear-resistant. It is 50 percent more absorbent than cotton, dyes well, is colorfast and resistant to pilling, shrinkage and fading. It is prone to wrinkling.

RAYON

Rayon manufacture is a long and involved process in which specially processed wood pulp is dissolved into liquid form using caustic soda, then extruded through a spinnerette in filaments, and finally reconstituted back into cellulose. The filaments are drawn out, or stretched, then washed to remove impurities, and finally are sent through a rotary cutter to cut the fibers into pieces that can be spun into yarn. Rayon is neither completely synthetic nor entirely natural.

Rayon was originally conceived as a substitute for silk in the 1800s. The process used to make rayon has been refined and updated many times. Today's rayon is "high-wet-modulus" (or HWM) rayon, a stronger and more durable fiber.

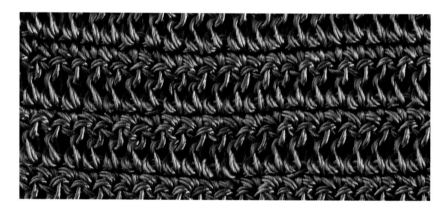

RAYON CHARACTERISTICS

Rayon is much heavier than silk, can have an intense sheen and drapes elegantly. It weakens when wet but firms up when dried. Rayon is cool and soft to wear, and the fiber takes dye easily. It is similar in comfort to all-natural fibers.

SOY

The soybean is a legume that has long been used in China. It has been domesticated for so long that its true origins are unknown. It is now an important crop worldwide.

Today, soy pulp, an extract of tofu production, is used to make high-quality textiles. In this process, liquefied protein is mechanically extruded into long fibers which are then cut and spun into yarn. The finished fiber is approximately 45 percent protein, which makes the fiber receptive to natural dyes. The fiber is 100 percent biodegradable.

The natural color of soy fiber is a soft ivory. Knitted fabrics made from soy have a hand similar to silk blended with cashmere, and have been referred to as vegetable cashmere. Fabrics have an elegant drape and a silky luster.

SOY CHARACTERISTICS
The fiber is soft, smooth, breathable, has better moisture transmission than cotton, retains warmth like wool and is naturally antimicrobial. The fiber strength is higher than cotton and wool, creating a stable fabric. It is washable, colorfast, not prone to shrinkage and resists creasing.

RECYCLED FIBER

Many fibers can be given a second life by being recycled into yarn. While any type of fiber can be used in recycled yarn, the fibers used in the yarn featured here are extruded. The idea of recycling is attractive to those who seek to reuse rather than harvest new materials.

BANANA SILK

Banana fabrics were common in Asia until cotton gained popularity. The current banana silk yarn is made from the waste from weaving mills, and is a modern rayon-type fiber.

Yarn made from banana fiber consists of recycled fiber called jusi that is used in sari weaving in India. Leftovers from weaving called thrums (strands of warp left over after a piece is cut from the loom) that would otherwise be thrown away are instead used to make yarn. Many of these yarns are Fair Trade Certified. There may be silk included in the fiber mix of some of these yarns.

BANANA SILK CHARACTERISTICS
An artisan yarn with lots of character, the skeins have no dye lots and are unevenly spun. It is a fuzzy yarn with high sheen, produced in a worsted or bulky weight, and it tends to be heavy. The yarns are kettle-dyed or hand painted and make a fabric that drapes beautifully.

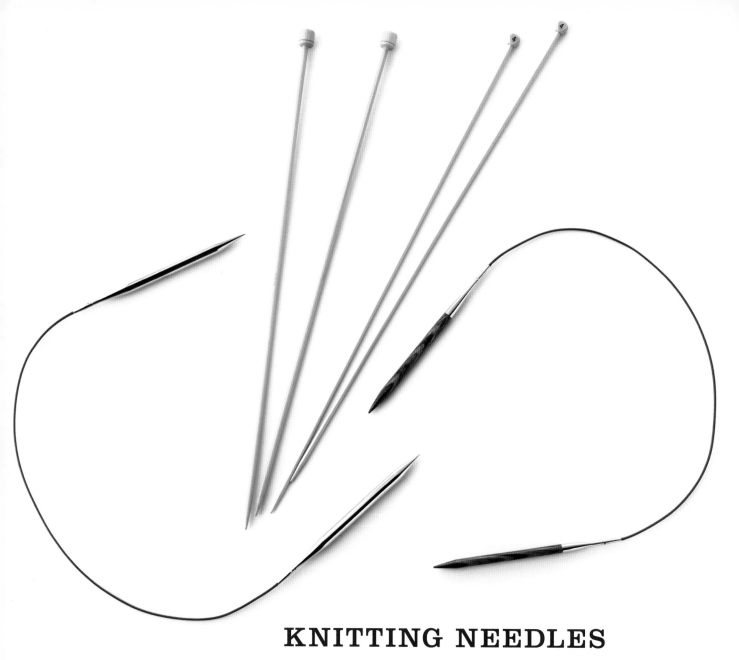

KNITTING NEEDLES

Any type of knitting needle can be used to knit plant-based yarns, although as you work your way through the different varieties, you will probably develop your own preferences. I have found that wood or bamboo needles seem to "fit" best with soft yarns such as soy and cotton, and also help keep slippery yarns in place. And I prefer metal needles to knit linen and hemp, the coarser yarns, because the metal is a better match to these sturdy fibers. Try different combinations of yarns and needles to find what works best for you.

Quality tools are crucial in doing precise work in any craft, and knitting is no exception. My favorites are nickel-plated needles that have fine points because they make maneuverability a breeze. A set of interchangeable circular needles is also a great investment—they offer lots of flexibility in cord lengths so you can adapt to any project, and you will never lack the correct needle size. There are other advantages to circular needles, as well, even if you're knitting flat. With circular knitting needles, there is less strain on your hands because the bulk of the project is centered over your lap, and dropped needles haven't far to go. Plus, your seat partner doesn't get jabbed with the flailing end of a straight needle.

OTHER TOOLS

There are a few other tools that are neccessary for the projects in this book, and a few more that you may find helpful, even though they aren't required. Use the ones you like, and feel free to leave behind the ones you don't need.

Crochet hooks are used in projects that are crocheted or combine knit and crochet, but you may find them handy for your knitting projects as well. They are great for fixing dropped stitches in knitting. Crochet hooks are available in a variety of sizes; you can find a helpful size chart on page 141. As with knitting needles, it is often helpful to have a complete set of crochet hooks so that you can easily change sizes to achieve your desired gauge.

A few other helpful tools are large-eyed blunt needles (called yarn needles or tapestry needles) and a small pair of very sharp scissors. The needles are used to sew up sweaters and sew in yarn ends, and scissors are used to snip the yarn ends. A stitch gauge or a ruler is used to accurately establish gauge, and a tape measure is needed when you want to measure the width and length of your knitting, or to accurately take measurements to achieve a good fit.

Other tools that you might find helpful are stitch markers, a row counter and a cable needle. Stitch markers are small rings that sit on your knitting needle and help you keep track of your pattern. A row counter also helps you keep track of where you are in a pattern. A cable needle is a short needle that can be used to hold stitches during the formation of a cable. These can be purchased from any store that sells knitting notions, or you can use anything that will hold the stitches as you work, such as a bobby pin. A stitch holder is also a useful tool that will securely hold stitches that aren't currently being worked.

For blocking your projects you will need a padded, waterproof surface, pins and a tape measure (see *Blocking a Garment*, page 22).

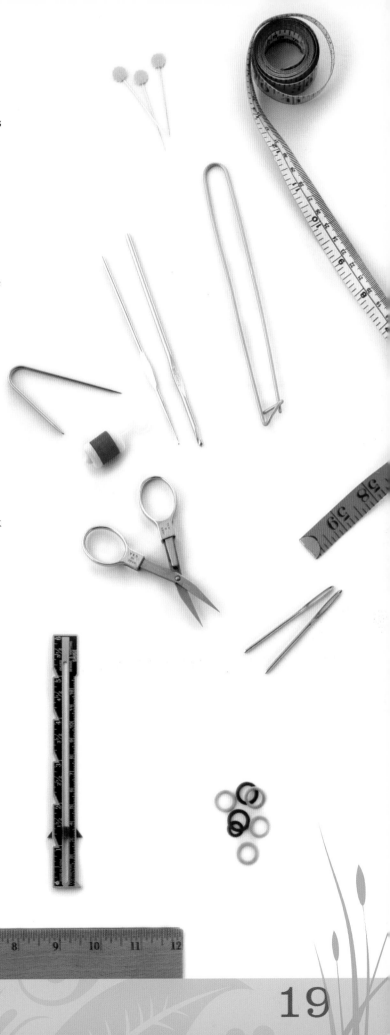

19

TIPS, TRICKS AND IMPORTANT INFORMATION

The following information will help you along on your plant-based knitting adventure. These tips and tricks will show you how to learn about a yarn before you start knitting and will see you through to finishing a new garment. From choosing a pattern stitch to making sure your garment turns out the correct size and shape, use this treasure trove of information to create successful projects you'll enjoy making and using.

BEFORE KNITTING

When a yarn is new to you, some preliminary background work is essential. Knit with the yarn until you have the "feel" of it. Sometimes just making a swatch is sufficient, but if not, keep knitting for awhile. A yarn's characteristics can vary greatly from one plant fiber to another,, so it is important to learn about it by knitting with it. When you are ready, prepare the swatch following the instructions below. Also pay attention to *Fitting a Sweater*, as this will help ensure that the finished garment will fit as you want it to.

PREPARING A SWATCH

This step is absolutely essential: Always make a swatch of a yarn you are not familiar with before knitting a garment with it. Use the swatch to find out how the knitted fabric behaves, to check for changes such as shrinkage or growth, and to measure the gauge.

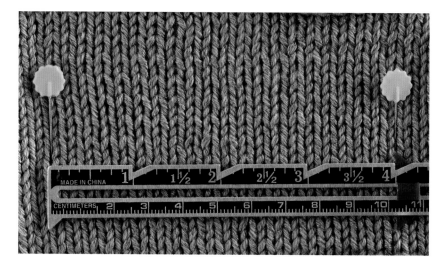

To prepare a swatch before beginning a new project, start with the yarn, needle size and pattern stitch recommended in the "Gauge" section of the pattern. Knit a swatch that is at least 4" × 4" (10cm × 10cm)—the larger, the better. Measure the width and length of the swatch and determine the gauge; write down all of this information for later reference. To find the gauge, lay the swatch flat (without stretching the fabric), lay a ruler horizontally across the swatch, and place pins in the swatch 4" (10cm) apart. Carefully count the stitches between the pins, including a half stitch at the end if there is one. Do the same vertically to count the rows.

After measuring, treat the swatch exactly as you would the finished project (see *After Knitting*, page 22); for instance, block or wash the swatch according to the yarn label instructions. For some yarns, blocking will entail washing the swatch and then letting it

dry. With linen, cotton and hemp yarns, I like to use an iron to speed the drying process by ironing on medium heat until the swatch is not quite dry, then allowing it to air-dry. Once the swatch is dry measure the width, length and gauge again. Record any changes and compare the measurements to the "Gauge" information provided with the pattern. Adjust your needle size if necessary to obtain the same gauge as given in the pattern.

If a sweater is knitted according to the washed/blocked gauge, it will become the correct size after washing and blocking. Some yarns will stay the same after finishing, while others will

shrink in one or both directions, and yet others will relax, becoming slightly wider. Shrinkage or relaxing happens only once, and should be considered a part of the process of making a beautiful and unique garment that can be worn for many years.

Besides sizing information, you can also learn much more from a swatch. You can see how the coloration of a yarn interacts with the stitch pattern. For instance, some variegated yarns will disguise an otherwise lovely stitch pattern. You can also learn about the stitch definition and resiliency of a yarn from a swatch.

STITCH DEFINITION

Stitch definition is the ability of a yarn to show stitch patterns in knitting. Some plant-based yarns will produce excellent stitch definition; smooth yarns will show stitches best. In other yarns, stitches tend to flatten out and the effect is more like a damask fabric than a dimensional one. Either can be an attractive look, but knowing which effect a yarn has is useful information. To see how a yarn will show off stitch patterns, make swatches of different stitch patterns, treat them as you would the finished project (washing, blocking, etc.), and assess the results. Here, the corn yarn sample (pink) retains the original stitch definition after washing, but the soy yarn (purple) has relaxed into a softer, damask-like surface.

RESILIENCY

Resiliency is a characteristic of some fibers that allows them to retain their shape and bounce back from wear and tear. This characteristic is lacking in plant-based yarns, which is the major difference between plant-based yarns and wool yarns. Some plant-based yarns, such as cotton, soy and bamboo, seem to have plenty of bounce while you are knitting. However, the process of washing, blocking and then wearing will flatten out some or all of this bounce. Soy and some other rayon-like yarns will relax with just a spritz of water so you can see this right away.

Ribbed cuffs and neck edges are often used in knitting to create shaping in a garment, but ribbing created with plant-based yarns will have a tendency to stretch out and stay that way instead of bouncing back. Use ribbing for stitch contrast instead of shaping, and find other ways to finish edges.

Finishes for edges can consist of ribbing (for decorative effect), seed stitch, garter stitch, curled Stockinette stitch, wavy effects created with extra stitches, the natural edges of lace patterns, turned-under hems, sewn-on knitted lace and crochet.

FITTING A SWEATER

Use the schematics and measurements included with the patterns in this book to choose the correct size to knit, or to modify a pattern for a perfect fit. The difference between the given size and the finished measurements tells how closely the sweater is designed to fit. If you prefer a looser fit, make a larger size; for a closer fit, knit a smaller size.

Some of these designs are shaped to fit at the waist. To check your measurements against those of the garment, tie a string around your waist. Measure from shoulder to waist and compare with the dimensions given on the pattern's schematic. If you are longer- or shorter-waisted, add or subtract rows to achieve the correct fit.

AFTER KNITTING

Once you've invested your time and creativity in a project, you want it to turn out just right. Finish your project using the following steps so that the parts will assemble into a beautiful garment. Pay attention to the washing instructions that come with the yarn. With proper care, any of the plant fibers can hold up to years of wear, and your lovingly made garment could even become a family heirloom.

WEAVING IN ENDS

After you've completed the knitting, the first finishing task is to weave loose ends into the wrong side of the work. Work into the backs of stitches and check that this is invisible from the front. Doubling back (weaving in one direction, then turning and weaving back the opposite way) helps to secure the ends of even the slipperiest yarns. If working intarsia, try to weave ends into a matching color.

WASHING KNITS

After weaving in ends, it is time to wash the knitted pieces. Always consult the yarn label for washing instructions. Some yarns may need special care; for instance, bamboo and rayon yarns tend to harden when they become wet, but soften again when dry. Most handknits can be washed by hand; treat your special knits well by hand washing in lukewarm water with a gentle, natural soap. Once the pieces are washed and all the soap is rinsed out, roll the pieces up in a towel to remove excess moisture, then dry flat. Block to shape if needed.

Many yarn labels now say that the knitted garment can be machine washed. Always machine wash your swatch first to see how the yarn handles this treatment. Some knits can even be dried in a dryer, but always take the piece out while it is still slightly damp, then air dry the rest of the way.

IRONING

Ironing is optional—knits don't usually require it. If you choose to iron a knit, always test-iron your swatch before ironing a finished garment; different yarns react in different ways to ironing. Ironing is not recommended for rayon-type yarns—it tends to severely squash the knitting—and corn yarns cannot be ironed at all because they will melt. Linen and hemp seem to thrive on ironing, although the knitted surface may gain a subtle sheen. If you want to maintain the yarn's original finish, use a press cloth or iron on the wrong side of the work. Cottons can be ironed with a bit of steam. Stop ironing when the fabric is still slightly damp and allow it to air dry the rest of the way—do not iron knits to the point that they dry completely.

BLOCKING A GARMENT

Most blocking is done after the pieces are knitted and not yet assembled. Some plant fiber yarns require blocking, while others do not need it. Follow any instructions given on the label. To block, begin by washing the garment pieces in the same manner as the swatch prepared for the project. Lay each piece out on a flat surface, then measure and form the piece using the schematic given in the pattern instructions. Some tightly spun yarns may skew as they are knitted: Dampen and shape the pieces by fastening into shape with pins onto a padded surface. Allow all pieces to dry completely (ironing can be used for cotton, linen, and hemp as stated earlier). Once blocking is complete, sew the pieces together according to instructions in the pattern.

CUSTOMIZING PROJECTS

While many wonderful commercial plant-based yarns are available, don't be afraid to add your own twist to the yarns to really make the project your own. Here are some suggestions for exploring the fibers in creative ways. Check with your local yarn shops and browse the Internet for more information on these topics. Create some original and unique yarns!

PLYING

Use a spinning wheel or spindle to create your own yarns by plying, or twisting, together different commercial yarns. Purchase coned yarns for machine knitting or weaving, hold two or more strands together and add twist with a spinning wheel or spindle. Plying yarns together is much more effective than simply holding yarn ends together and knitting them. The yarn will knit more easily and if yarns of different colors are combined, they will be evenly distributed.

SPINNING

Many plant-based fibers are available for spinning. With these you can custom-make your own unique yarns using a spinning wheel or spindle.

DYEING

Dyeing is another way to produce unique yarns. Create solid, mottled, or space-dyed hanks of yarn. For soy-based yarns, choose dyes and dye assists meant for protein-based fibers. For all other plant-based yarns and fibers, choose dyes and dye assists meant for cellulose-based fibers.

CROCHET

Crochet is applied to many of the sweaters in this book because it makes a great edging. It defines the edges, holds up to wear without stretching, and blends well with knitting. *Midnight Flowers*, a crochet mesh scarf on page 86, shows the versatility of crochet. Worked in fine yarn with a small crochet hook, it shows how crochet can be used to create defined shapes with interior dimension.

If your skill is in knitting, then you have already mastered the more challenging of the two. Crochet is simple to do and easy to learn. Someone who knows how can teach you, or follow the steps in a how-to book. Learn one stitch—the single crochet—and you can crochet an edging onto a knitted sweater.

MACHINE KNITTING

For quicker garment production, a knitting machine can also be used with plant-based yarns. Basic knitting machines can create knitted fabrics in Stockinette stitch. Machine-knitted ribbings or laces can be done with additional equipment. Techniques such as increasing, decreasing, binding off and cables can be done by manipulating the stitches by hand. With a fine-gauge knitting machine it is easy and quick to make luxurious, finely knit garments. Bamboo, Lyocell, cotton, linen and other yarns are available on cones for machine knitting. A mid-gauge knitting machine can also be used with many of the skeined yarns, although the yarns must be specially wound so the end will move freely from the skein. Some of the coarser bast fiber yarns may not work well on some knitting machines.

PATTERNS

In this section I present styles to live, work and play in, to go out on the town in, and to wear during every season. Here you can find styles that you will enjoy both knitting and wearing. Explore the gorgeous and wearable fibers that are derived from plants and find your favorites.

Try luxurious linen on fine needles to make a sweet camisole, such as *Flax* on page 74. Or, use large needles to knit hemp to make *Wild Blueberry*, a lovely shawl on page 66. Cable lovers can get cable-happy with *Chocolate Dust*, a bamboo capelet suitable for an evening at the opera, on page 58. Lace knitters may enjoy making the summery cotton top *Traveling Vine* on page 112, the linen and cotton cropped cardigan *Maiden's Blush* on page 108, or the beaded rayon sweater *Dew on Lilac* on page 46.

Crocheters will find projects here, as well. Add a new, beautiful piece to your wardrobe with the linen and cotton scarf *Midnight Flowers* on page 86. Accessorize with a hemp belt like *Silver Saxifrage* on page 56 or a rayon purse like *Autumn Oak Leaf* on page 124. You can also combine knit and crochet to make a cotton top like *Sage* on page 104, perfect for warm summer days.

For winter, try a cozy Fair Isle sweater in soy like *The Forest for the Trees* on page 40. A snuggly soft pillbox-style hat like *Cotton Boll* on page 128 will keep you both warm and fashionable.

Whatever you decide to make, enjoy this garden of designs for plant-based yarns.

MOUNTAIN FLORA

Mountains upon mountains as far as the eye can see … and all created from cotton in gorgeous natural colors. From rich, mossy greens to sumptuous golds and browns, these colors are a feast for the eyes. The wonderful softness of organic cotton yarn and generous sizing make this a comfortable man's vest or woman's summer top.

SKILL LEVEL
Intermediate

METHOD
Knit

SIZES
To fit actual bust or chest size: 36 (40, 44, 48)" (91 [102, 112, 122]cm)

FINISHED MEASUREMENTS
Bust or chest: Approx 42¼ (46½, 50¼, 56)" (107 [118, 128, 142]cm)

YARN
15 (25, 26, 36) (1¾ oz./50g, 88 yd./80m) skeins worsted weight yarn, 5 (5, 6, 6) skeins MC, 1 (2, 2, 3) skeins each of 10 colors (CC1, CC2, CC3, CC4, CC5, CC6, CC7, CC8, CC9, CC10)

NEEDLES
Size US 7 (4.5mm) straight needles

Size US 6 (4mm) straight needles

Size US 4 (3.5mm) straight needles

If necessary, change needle size to obtain correct gauge.

NOTIONS
Bobbins

Yarn needle

GAUGE
16 sts and 26 rows = 4" (10cm) in St st on size US 7 (4.5mm) needles

The project shown at right was made using Ecobutterfly Pakucho (100% certified organic cotton, 1¾ oz./50g, 88 yd./80m) in Dark Chocolate (MC), Vanilla Cream (CC1), Vicuna (CC2), Cafe (CC3), Deep Golden Brown (CC4), Moka Chocolate (CC5), Chocolate (CC6), Sage (CC7), Rustic Avocado (CC8), Forest Mist (CC9) and Deep Green (CC10).

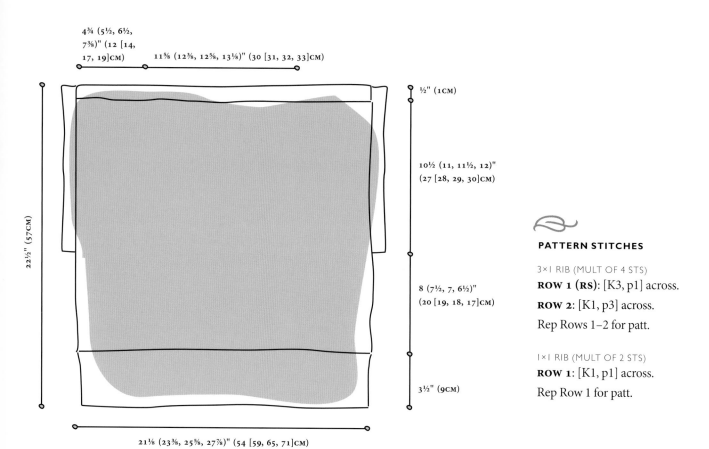

4¾ (5½, 6½, 7⅜)" (12 [14, 17, 19]cm)

11⅝ (12⅜, 12⅝, 13⅛)" (30 [31, 32, 33]cm)

½" (1cm)

10½ (11, 11½, 12)" (27 [28, 29, 30]cm)

22½" (57cm)

8 (7½, 7, 6½)" (20 [19, 18, 17]cm)

3½" (9cm)

21⅛ (23⅜, 25⅝, 27⅞)" (54 [59, 65, 71]cm)

PATTERN STITCHES

3×1 RIB (MULT OF 4 STS)

ROW 1 (RS): [K3, p1] across.

ROW 2: [K1, p3] across.

Rep Rows 1–2 for patt.

1×1 RIB (MULT OF 2 STS)

ROW 1: [K1, p1] across.

Rep Row 1 for patt.

Back

Using size 6 needles and MC, CO 76 (84, 92, 100) sts.

NEXT ROW (WS): Work Row 2 of 3×1 Rib.

NEXT ROW (RS): Work Row 1 of 3×1 Rib.

Cont in 3×1 Rib patt for 3½" (9cm).

NEXT ROW (RS): Change to size 7 needles and St st, and inc 8 (8, 10, 10) sts evenly across next row—84 (92, 102, 110) sts.

Work even in MC for 1" (3cm) more, then beg Colorwork Chart (use the appropriate chart for the size you are knitting).

Note: Use the Intarsia method to work this portion, with a separate ball or bobbin of yarn for ea color area. There will be some areas where colors can be stranded as in the Fair Isle technique—strand only for short distances to avoid long floats.

When charted section is complete, change to size 4 needles and MC. Work in 1×1 Rib for 1" (3cm). BO in patt.

Front

Work as for Back, reversing Colorwork Chart. (When sewn tog the mountains will be continuous from Front to Back of sweater).

Finishing

Weave in all ends. Block pieces if needed. Sew Shoulders tog, overlapping the ribbings. Ease the overlap over 4¾ (5½, 6½, 7⅜)" (12 [14, 17, 19]cm) on ea side, leaving center open for neck. Sew the ends securely.

Armhole Trim

Using size 6 needles and MC, pick up and k 80 (84, 88, 92) sts over 11 (11½, 12, 12½)" (28 [29, 30, 32]cm) on both the Front and Back sections (centered at Shoulder) and along the edges of the Shoulder ribbings, working through both layers there. Work in 3×1 Rib for 1" (3cm). BO in patt. Sew side seams, including bottoms of Armhole Trim. Weave in remaining ends.

Embroidery

With MC, work backstitching along edges of mountains. Add additional Embroidery as desired; here, I backstitched lines on some of the mountains, placed scattered French knots on some and left others plain.

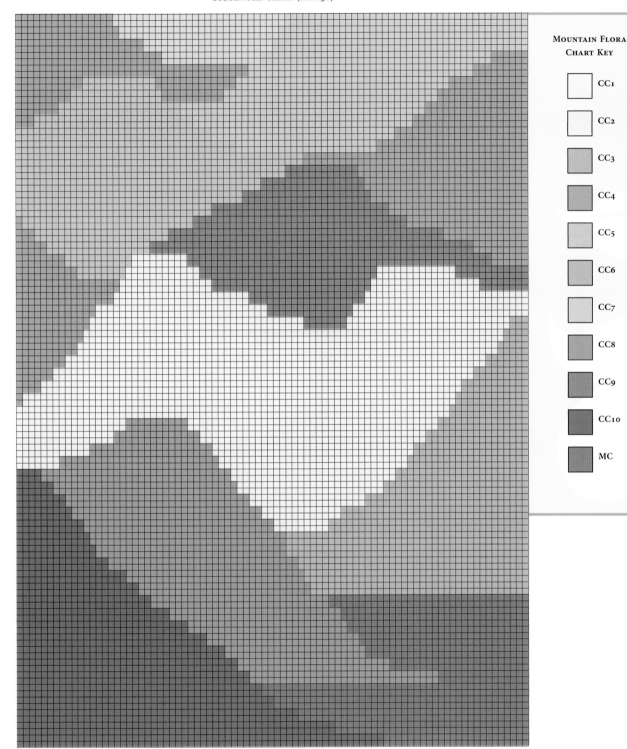

MOUNTAIN FLORA
CHART KEY

CC1

CC2

CC3

CC4

CC5

CC6

CC7

CC8

CC9

CC10

MC

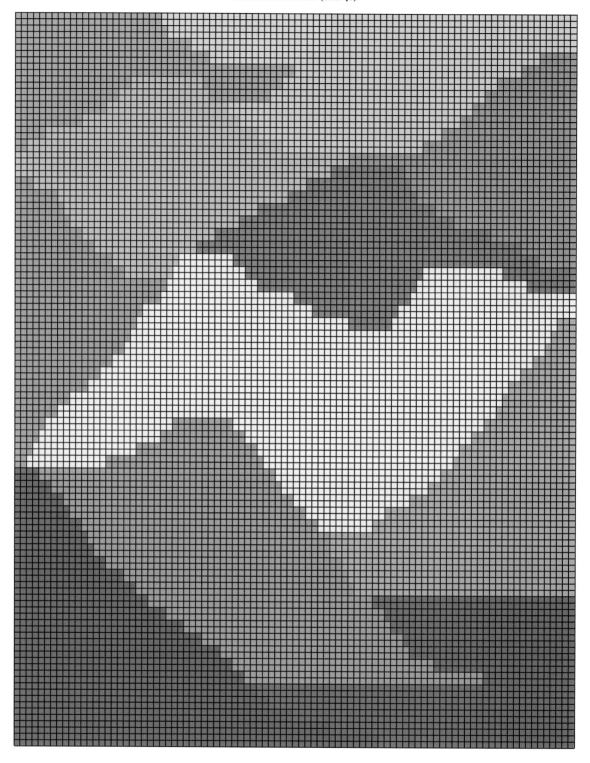

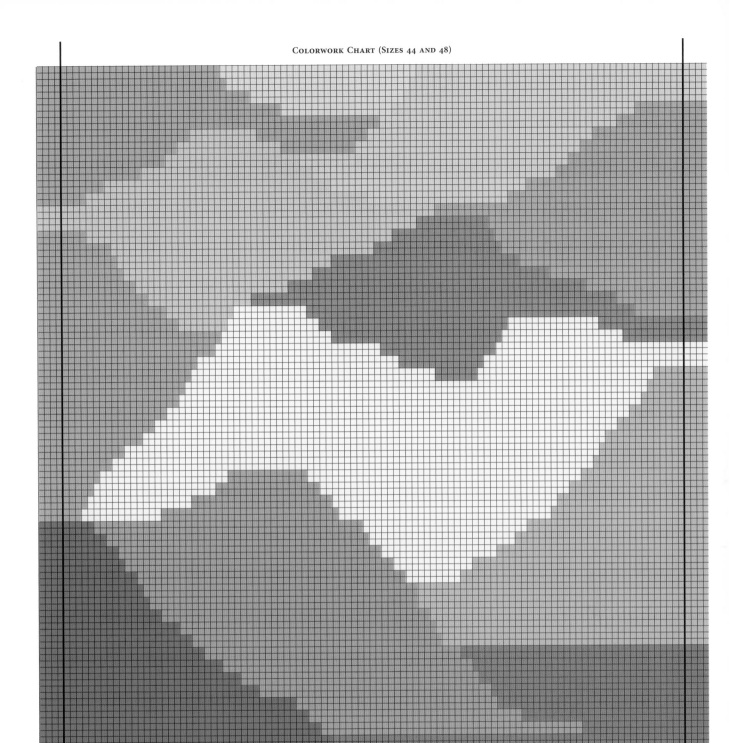

Size 48

Size 44

Size 48

LIME PEEL

This easy-wear boat neck pullover features a cable panel set into a background of Reverse Stockinette stitch with an isolated cable on the front, back and one sleeve. I wanted to knit this sweater with a pure Lyocell yarn, but could not find one in worsted weight. I ended up customizing my own yarn for this sweater by plying strands of commercial yarn together, but there are many gauge-friendly substitutions available.

SKILL LEVEL
Experienced

METHOD
Knit and Crochet

SIZES
To fit actual bust size: 32 (34, 36, 39, 42, 46)" (81 [86, 91, 99, 107, 117]cm)

FINISHED MEASUREMENTS
Bust: Approx 36 (39, 41½, 44½, 48, 52¼)" (91 [99, 105, 113, 122, 133]cm)

YARN
12 (12, 13, 13, 14, 15) (1¾ oz./50g, 109 yd./100m) skeins worsted weight yarn

NEEDLES
Size US 5 (3.75mm) straight needles

If necessary, change needle size to obtain correct gauge.

HOOK
Size US F/5 (3.75mm) crochet hook

NOTIONS
Stitch markers

Cable needle

Yarn needle

GAUGE
20 sts and 28 rows = 4" (10cm) in St st

Cable Panel: 8¼" (21cm) wide

The project shown at right was made using Valley Yarns 8/2 Tencel (100% Tencel, 16 oz./453g, 3360 yd./3072m) in Lemongrass plied to create a 4-strand yarn. Cascade Pima Tencel (50% Pima cotton/50% Tencel, 1¾ oz./50g, 109 yd./100m) in color 8374 is a suitable replacement.

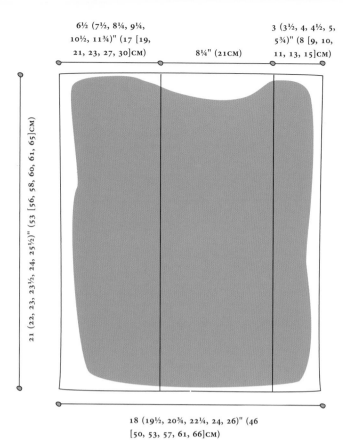

6½ (7½, 8¼, 9¼, 10½, 11¾)" (17 [19, 21, 23, 27, 30]CM)   8¼" (21CM)   3 (3½, 4, 4½, 5, 5¾)" (8 [9, 10, 11, 13, 15]CM)

21 (22, 23, 23½, 24, 25½)" (53 [56, 58, 60, 61, 65]CM)

18 (19½, 20¾, 22¼, 24, 26)" (46 [50, 53, 57, 61, 66]CM)

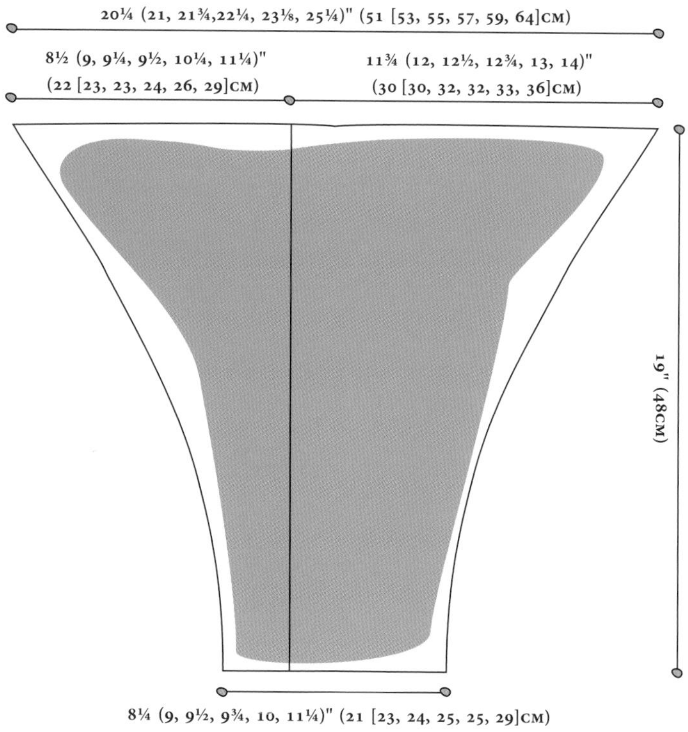

20¼ (21, 21¾,22¼, 23⅛, 25¼)" (51 [53, 55, 57, 59, 64]CM)

8½ (9, 9¼, 9½, 10¼, 11¼)" (22 [23, 23, 24, 26, 29]CM)   11¾ (12, 12½, 12¾, 13, 14)" (30 [30, 32, 32, 33, 36]CM)

19" (48CM)

8¼ (9, 9½, 9¾, 10, 11¼)" (21 [23, 24, 25, 25, 29]CM)

ABBREVIATIONS

C4F/K1/K4
Slip 4 sts to cn and hold to front, k1, k4 from cn.

C4F/P1/K4
Slip 4 sts to cn and hold to front, p1, k4 from cn.

C1B/K4/K1
Slip 1 st to cn and hold to back, k4, k1 from cn.

C1B/K4/P1
Slip 1 st to cn and hold to back, k4, p1 from cn.

C3F/K1/K3
Slip 3 sts to cn and hold to front, k1, k3 from cn.

C4B/K4/K4
Slip 4 sts to cn and hold to back, k4, k4 from cn.

C4F/K4/K4
Slip 4 sts to cn and hold to front, k4, k4 from cn.

PATTERN STITCHES

REVERSE STOCKINETTE STITCH (MULT OF 1 ST)
ROW 1 (RS): P all sts.
ROW 2: K all sts.
Rep Rows 1–2 for patt.

CABLE PANEL (WORKED OVER 64 STS)
SET-UP ROW (WS): P4, *k8, p8; rep from * 3 times, end k8, p4.
ROW 1 (RS): C4F/K1/K4, *p6, C1B/K4/K1, C4F/K1/K4; rep from * 3 times, end p6, C1B/K4/K1.
ROW 2 (AND ALL WS ROWS): K the p sts and p the k sts of the prev row.
ROW 3: K1, C4F/K1/K4, *p4, C1B/K4/K1, k2, C4F/K1/K4; rep from * 3 times, end p4, C1B/K4/K1, k1.
ROW 5: K2, C4F/P1/K4, *p2, C1B/K4/P1, k4, C4F/P1/K4; rep from * 3 times, end p2, C1B/K4/P1, k2.
ROW 7: K2, p1, *C4F/P1/K4, C1B/K4/P1, p1, k4, p1; rep from * 3 times, end C4F/P1/K4, C1B/K4/P1, p1, k2.
ROW 9: K2, p2, *C4B/K4/K4, p2, k4, p2; rep from * 3 times, end C4B/K4/K4, p2, k2.
ROW 11: K2, p1, *C1B/K4/P1, C4F/P1/K4, p1, k4, p1; rep from * 3 times, end C1B/K4/P1, C4F/P1/K4, p1, k2.
ROW 13: K2, *C1B/K4/P1, p2, C4F/P1/K4, k4; rep from * 3 times, end C1B/K4/P1, p2, C4F/P1/K4, k2.
ROW 15: K1, *C1B/K4/P1, p4, C4F/P1/K4, k2; rep from * 3 times, end C1B/K4/P1, p4, C4F/P1/K4, k1.
ROW 17: *C1B/K4/P1, p6, C4F/P1/K4; rep from * across.
ROW 19: C3F/K1/K3, *p8, C4F/K4/K4; rep from * 3 times, end p8, C3F/K1/K3.
Rep Rows 1–20 for patt.

ISOLATED CABLE (WORKED OVER 10 STS)

SET-UP ROW (WS): On same row as Row 6 of Cable Panel: P4, k2, p4.

ROW 1 (RS): On same row as Row 7 of Cable Panel: C4F/P1/K4, C1B/K4/P1.

ROWS 2, 4 AND 6 (WS): On same rows as Rows 8, 10 and 12 of Cable Panel: K the p and p the k sts of the prev row.

ROW 3: On same row as Row 9 of Cable Panel: P1, C4B/K4/K4, p1.

ROW 5: On same row as Row 11 of Cable Panel: C1B/K4/P1, C4F/P1/K4.

ROW 7: On same row as Row 12 of Cable Panel: P all sts. Cont in Reverse Stockinette Stitch until Row 6 of Cable Panel, then rep Isolated Cable patt.

Front

CO 111 (120, 126, 132, 141, 150) sts.

ROW 1 (WS): K32 (38, 42, 46, 52, 58) sts, work Set-Up Row of Cable Panel, k15 (18, 20, 22, 25, 28) sts.

ROW 2 (RS): Work Row 1 of Reverse Stockinette Stitch to Cable Panel, work Row 1 of Cable Panel, work Row 1 of Reverse Stockinette Stitch to end of row.

ROWS 3–5: Cont to work Cable Panel as est and sts on both sides in Reverse Stockinette Stitch.

ROW 6 OF CABLE PANEL (WS): Beg the row as est through the Cable Panel sts, then k16 (19, 21, 23, 26, 29) sts, work next 10 sts in Row 1 of Isolated Cable, k6 (9, 11, 13, 16, 19) sts.

Cont in patt as est for 21 (22, 23, 23½, 24, 25½)" (53 [56, 58, 60, 61, 65]cm). End the sweater front after Row 17 of Cable Panel. BO all sts.

Back

Work as for Front, reversing the placement of Cable Panel and Isolated Cable so the cable patterns will align at the top of the finished sweater, as foll:

ROW 1 (WS): K15 (18, 20, 22, 25, 28) sts, work Set-Up Row of Cable Panel, k32 (38, 42, 46, 52, 58) sts.

Right Sleeve

Beg at the top of the Sleeve and CO 102 (105, 108, 112, 116, 126) sts.

ROW 1 (WS): K all sts.

ROW 2 (RS): P all sts.

Cont in Reverse Stockinette Stitch, beg Sleeve shaping:

Dec 1 st at ea end of every RS row 17 (17, 18, 18, 18, 22) times—68 (71, 72, 76, 80, 82) sts.

Then dec 1 st at ea end of row every 4 rows 4 (4, 4, 5, 6, 8) times—60 (63, 64, 66, 64, 66) sts.

Then dec 1 st at ea end of row every 6 rows 9 (9, 9, 9, 9, 5) times—42 (45, 46, 48, 50, 56) sts.

Work even until Right Sleeve meas 19" (48cm). BO all sts.

Left Sleeve

Work as for Right Sleeve, including all shaping. AT THE SAME TIME, work as foll:

ROW 6 (WS): K38 (35, 39, 41, 44, 49) sts, work Row 1 of Isolated Cable across next 10 sts, knit to end. (If needed, use a stitch marker, slipping it every row in order to keep the cables in line for length of Sleeve). Cont to work the 7 rows of Isolated Cable as est, then work 13 rows plain. Rep Isolated Cable directly in line with earlier cable. Cont the row of Isolated Cables to cuff end of Sleeve. Work as est until Sleeve meas 19" (48cm). BO all sts.

Note: Sleeve should end several rows past a completed Isolated Cable. If your sleeve is ending anywhere in the midst of one, eliminate the final cable.

Finishing

Weave in ends. Block pieces. Sew Front and Back tog at Shoulders, leaving approx 11" (28cm) for neck (adjust for your preference). Sew Sleeves to Front and Back, then sew Sleeve and side seams.

Using size US F/5 crochet hook, work a row of sl st along edges of Sleeves, bottom of sweater and around neck. Weave in remaining ends.

PLUM AND PERSIMMON

You'll want to wear this cardigan next to your skin because the yarn feels so silky and soft. The Modal in this yarn adds a draping quality that cotton lacks, lending a touch of elegance to this sweater. Knitting from the top down will make it easy to match the stripes and to adjust the length of the sweater as you desire. For a cute, cropped look, end this sweater at the waist.

SKILL LEVEL
Advanced Beginner

METHOD
Knit

SIZES
To fit actual bust size: 31½ (34, 36, 39, 42)" (80 [86, 91, 99, 107]cm)

FINISHED MEASUREMENTS
Bust: Approx 36½ (39½, 42, 45, 48½)" (93 [100, 107, 114, 123]cm)

YARN
12 (12, 14, 14, 16) (1¾ oz./50g, 110 yd./101m) skeins sport weight yarn, 6 (6, 7, 7, 8) skeins each of 2 colors (MC and CC)

NEEDLES
Size US 4 (3.5mm) straight needles

NOTIONS
Yarn needle

6 buttons, ¾" (2cm) diameter

Row counter (optional)

GAUGE
20 sts and 28 rows = 4" (10cm)

The project shown at right was made using Knit Picks Shine Sport, (60% Pima cotton/40% Modal, 1¾ oz./50g, 110 yd./101m) in Terracotta (MC) and Violet (CC).

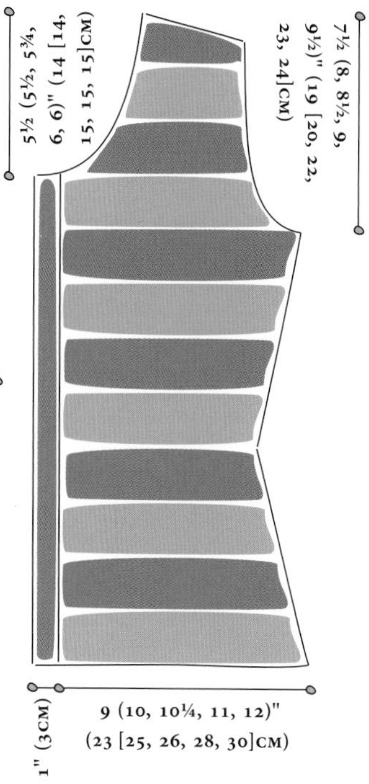
5½ (5½, 5¾, 6, 6)" (14 [14, 15, 15, 15]CM)
7½ (8, 8½, 9, 9½)" (19 [20, 22, 23, 24]CM)
1" (3CM)
9 (10, 10¼, 11, 12)"
(23 [25, 26, 28, 30]CM)

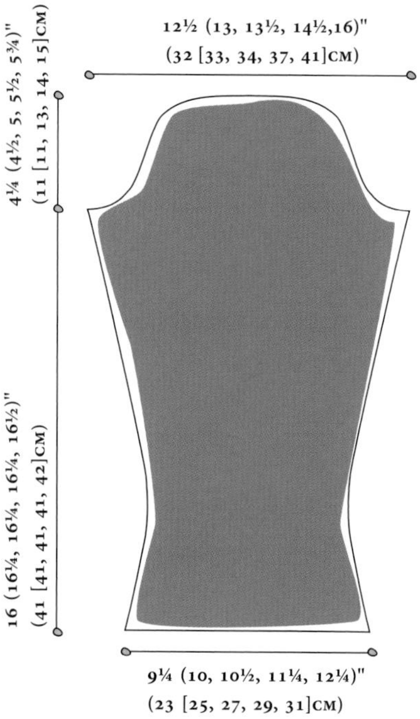
12½ (13, 13½, 14½,16)"
(32 [33, 34, 37, 41]CM)
4¼ (4½, 5, 5½, 5¾)" (11 [11, 13, 14, 15]CM)
16 (16¼, 16¼, 16¼, 16½)" (41 [41, 41, 41, 42]CM)
9¼ (10, 10½, 11¼, 12¼)"
(23 [25, 27, 29, 31]CM)

PATTERN STITCHES

KNITTED LACE EDGING

Using size 4 needles, CO 7 sts.

ROW 1: K1, yo, k2tog, k1, [yo] twice, k2tog, k1—8 sts.

ROW 2: Sl1, p1, k then p into double yo, p4.

ROW 3: K1, yo, k2tog, k3, [yo] twice, k2—10 sts.

ROW 4: Sl1, p1, k then p into double yo, p6.

ROW 5: K1, yo, k2tog, k1, [yo] twice, k2tog, k4—11 sts.

ROW 6: Sl1, p4, k then p into double yo, p4.

ROW 7: K1, yo, k2tog, k8—11 sts.

ROW 8: BO 4 kwise, p6.

Rep Rows 1–8 for patt. Once lace is required length, or slightly longer, end on Row 8. Ease the lace as it is sewn on.

1×1 RIB (MULT OF 2 STS)

ROW 1: *K1, p1; rep from * across.

Rep Row 1 for patt.

COLOR SEQUENCE

Use a row counter if needed. For Fronts and Back of sweater work 14 rows in MC, and 14 rows in CC; rep throughout. At the bottom of ea piece, end with a full 14 rows of the color in use.

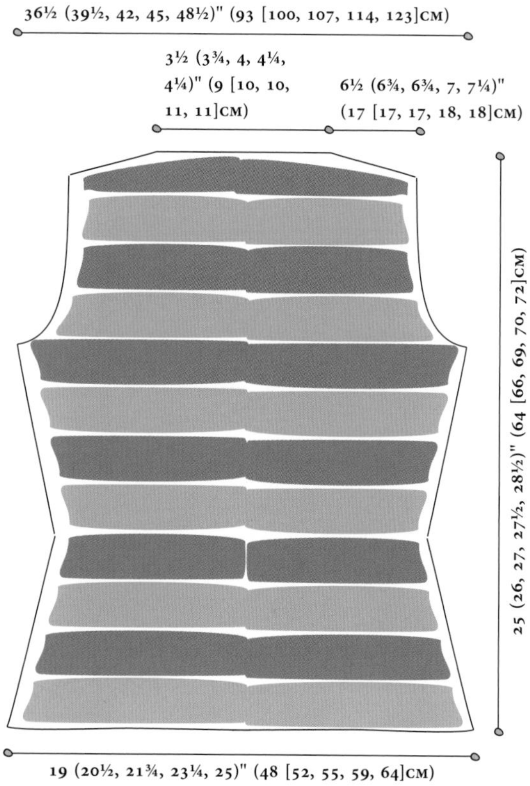
36½ (39½, 42, 45, 48½)" (93 [100, 107, 114, 123]CM)
3½ (3¾, 4, 4¼, 4¼)" (9 [10, 10, 11, 11]CM)
6½ (6¾, 6¾, 7, 7¼)" (17 [17, 17, 18, 18]CM)
25 (26, 27, 27½, 28½)" (64 [66, 69, 70, 72]CM)
19 (20½, 21¾, 23¼, 25)" (48 [52, 55, 59, 64]CM)

Left Front

With MC, CO 4 (4, 8, 8, 8) sts.

ROW 1 (RS): K all sts.

ROW 2: CO 6 (6, 5, 5, 5) sts and p across.

ROW 3: K all sts.

ROW 4: CO 5 (5, 5, 5, 5) sts and p across.

ROW 5: K all sts.

ROW 6: CO 4 (5, 3, 4, 4) sts and p across—19 (20, 21, 22, 22) sts.

Work even in St st, maintaining Color Sequence, for 1¼" (3cm), ending with a WS row.

Neck Shaping

Cont in St st, beg shaping:

Inc 1 st at beg of this and then every 4th (4th, 6th, 6th, 4th) row 3 (3, 3, 3, 5) times more—23 (24, 26, 26, 28) sts.

Then inc 1 st at Neck edge every RS row 3 (3, 3, 3, 3) times—26 (27, 29, 29, 31) sts.

Then, every other row, at Neck edge, inc 2 (2, 2, 2, 2) sts, then 2 (2, 2, 2, 2) sts, then 2 (3, 3, 4, 3) sts—32 (34, 36, 37, 38) sts.

Work even in St st, maintaining Color Sequence, until piece meas 5½ (5½, 6¼, 6¼, 6¼)" (14 [14, 16, 16, 16]cm) from top of Shoulder.

Armhole Shaping
At side edge, inc 1, then inc 1 again when Armhole meas 6 (6, 6¾, 6¾, 7)" (15 [15, 17, 17, 18]cm). For all sizes except 42, inc again when Armhole meas 6¼ (6½, 7, 7¾, –)" (16 [17, 18, 20, –]cm)—35 (37, 39, 40, 40) sts.

Inc 1 st at Armhole edge every other row 2 (2, 3, 3, 3) times, then inc 2 (2, 2, 4, 2) sts every other row once, then inc 4 (5, 5, 6, 2) sts every other row once. For size 42 only: then 2 sts, then 3 sts, then 5 sts every other row—43 (46, 49, 53, 57) sts.

Waist Shaping
Work even until piece meas 8 (9, 9, 9½, 10½)" (20 [23, 23, 24, 27]cm) from top of Shoulder. At side edge, dec 1 st on next row, then every 6th row 6 times—36 (39, 42, 46, 50) sts.

When piece meas 15½ (16, 17, 17¼, 17½)" (39 [41, 43, 44, 44]cm), work as foll: inc 1 st at side edge on next row, then every 6th row 8 (9, 9, 9, 9) times more—45 (49, 52, 56, 60) sts.

Work even until piece meas 25 (26, 27, 27½, 28½)" (64 [66, 69, 70, 72]cm), ending after completing a full 14 row color rep. BO all sts.

Right Front
With MC, CO 4 (4, 8, 8, 8) sts.

ROW 1: K all sts.

ROW 2: P all sts.

ROW 3: Beg CO for Shoulder shaping, and cont as for Left Front, reversing all shaping.

Back
CO 30 (32, 32, 34, 34) sts and foll the Shoulder, Armhole, and Waist shaping (ignore Neck shaping) same as for Fronts, working both sides of the Back at the same time.

At end of Shoulder shaping—68 (72, 76, 78, 80) sts.

At end of Armhole—90 (96, 102, 110, 118) sts. Check that Color Sequence matches the Fronts at the bottom of the Armhole.

At Waist—76 (82, 88, 96, 104) sts.

At bottom of Back—94 (102, 108, 116, 124) sts.

BO all sts.

Sleeves

Sleeve Cap
With MC for one Sleeve and CC for the other, CO 30 (30, 30, 34, 34) sts.

Inc 1 st at ea end of every RS row 2 (3, 3, 3, 4) times—34 (36, 36, 40, 42) sts.

Work 2 rows even, then inc 1 st at ea end of every RS row 5 (4, 5, 5, 4) times—44 (44, 46, 50, 50) sts.

Inc 1 st at ea end of next row, then inc 2 (1, 1, 1, 1) sts at ea end of next row, then inc 2 (1, 1, 2, 2) sts at ea end of next row, then inc 4 (3, 3, 3, 2) sts at ea end of next row, then inc 0 (4, 4, 4, 2) sts at ea end of next row 0 (1, 1, 1, 1) times.

SIZE 42 ONLY: Inc 3 sts at ea end of next row, then inc 4 sts at ea end of next row—62 (64, 66, 66, 72, 80) sts at bottom of Sleeve Cap.

Work even for ½" (1cm), then dec 1 st at ea end of next row, and at ea end of row every 6th row thereafter until 42 (48, 50, 52, 56) sts rem—20 (16, 16, 20, 24) sts dec.

When piece meas 18 (18, 18, 19, 20)" (46 [46, 46, 48, 51]cm), inc 1 st at ea end of next row and then at ea end of row every 6th row 2 (1, 1, 2, 2) times—48 (52, 54, 58, 62) sts.

Work even until piece meas 20¼ (20¾, 21¼, 21¾, 22¼)" (51 [53, 54, 55, 57]cm). BO all sts.

Finishing
Weave in ends. Block Fronts, Back and Sleeves. Make Knitted Lace Edging in MC and in CC to match bottom edge of ea Sleeve; sew in place. Sew Fronts to Back at Shoulder seams. Sew Sleeves into Armholes, easing if needed, then sew Sleeve and side seams. With the color that matches the bottom stripe of the sweater body, make Knitted Lace Edging to fit the bottom of the sweater and sew in place. With CC and RS facing, pick up and k 5 sts per 1" (3cm) around the Neck opening, then BO on the foll row.

Front Bands
With CC and RS facing, along Left Front opening, pick up and k 5 sts per 1" (3cm), 1 st on the Neck band, and 4 sts on the side of the bottom lace border. Work in 1×1 Rib for 1" (3cm), then BO in patt. Sew buttons on Left Front, placing the top button ¾" (2cm) from the upper edge, and the bottom button 1" (3cm) from the lower edge. Space rem buttons evenly between. Pick up and k as before along Right Front opening, and work in 1×1 Rib for ¼" (6mm). On next row, BO 2 sts opposite ea button for buttonholes. On next row, CO 2 sts over ea gap. Work even until Band meas 1" (3cm). BO in patt. Weave in remaining ends.

THE FOREST FOR THE TREES

Silky, soft soy yarn is a natural for Fair Isle patterning, and is used to good effect in this sweater. This man's or woman's design is inspired by the shapes of trees. The sweater is worked in the round up to the armholes, then back and forth on straight needles.

SKILL LEVEL
Experienced

METHOD
Knit

SIZES
To fit actual bust or chest size: 36 (42, 48)" (91 [107, 122]cm)

FINISHED MEASUREMENTS
Bust or chest: Approx 42 (48, 54)" (107 [122, 137]cm)

YARN
10 (12, 16) (1¾ oz./50g, 164 yd./150m) skeins DK weight yarn, 4 (5, 6) skeins MC, 3 (4, 5) skeins CC1, 2 (2, 3) skeins each of 4 colors (CC2, CC3, CC4, CC5), 1 (1, 2) skeins each of 2 colors (CC6, CC7)

NEEDLES
Size US 4 (3.5mm) straight needles

Size US 5 (3.75mm) straight needles

40" (100cm) size US 5 (3.75mm) circular needle

If necessary, change needle size to obtain correct gauge.

NOTIONS
Stitch markers

Stitch holder

Yarn needle

GAUGE
24 sts and 24 rows = 4" (10cm) on size US 5 (3.75mm) needles in Fair Isle patt. To establish gauge, work a swatch foll the color chart.

The project shown at right was made using South West Trading Company Pure (100% soy silk, 1¾ oz./50g, 164 yd./150m) in Blue Depths (MC), Walnut (CC1), Glacier (CC2), Northern Lights (CC3), Hickory (CC4), Iced Coffee (CC5), Marigold (CC6) and Snow (CC7).

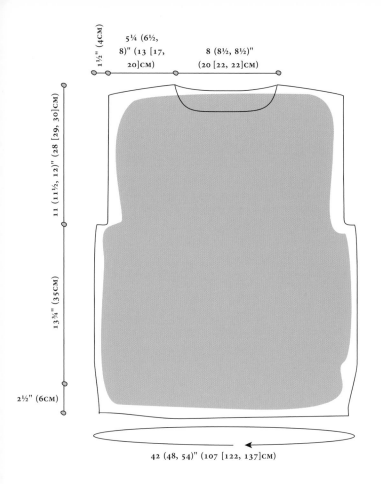

5¼ (6½, 8)" (13 [17, 20]CM)

1½" (4CM)

8 (8½, 8½)" (20 [22, 22]CM)

11 (11½, 12)" (28 [29, 30]CM)

13¾" (35CM)

2½" (6CM)

42 (48, 54)" (107 [122, 137]CM)

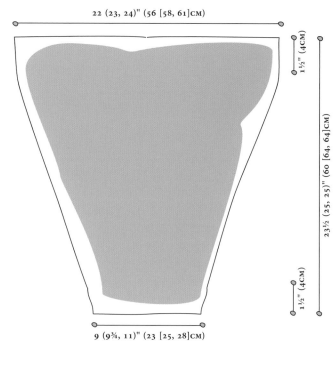

22 (23, 24)" (56 [58, 61]CM)

1½" (4CM)

23½ (25, 25)" (60 [64, 64]CM)

1½" (4CM)

9 (9¾, 11)" (23 [25, 28]CM)

PATTERN STITCHES

CORRUGATED RIB (MULT OF 3 STS)

ROW/RND 1 (RS): [K2 in CC1, p1 in CC5] around, stranding the unused color on WS.

ROW 2 (WORKING BACK AND FORTH ONLY): [K1 in CC5, p2 in CC1], stranding the unused color on WS.

Rep Rnd 1 for patt in circular knitting. When working flat, work Rep Rows 1–2 for patt.

Front and Back

Using size 4 circular needle and CC5, beg at the lower edge of Front and Back and CO 228 (258, 291) sts. Place marker and join in the rnd, taking care not to twist the sts. Join CC1 and work in Corrugated Rib for 1¼" (3cm). Cut yarns.

Join MC and CC3 and work 8 rnds of Chart 1, inc 12 (15, 15) sts evenly spaced along first rnd—240 (273, 306) sts.

Work 1 rnd in MC, inc 12 (15, 18) sts evenly spaced along the rnd—252 (288, 324) sts.

Change to size 5 circular needle and work 1 rnd in CC4, then beg Chart 2; keep marker at beg of rnd and add a second marker after 7th (8th, 9th) rep of charted pattern. Work to top of chart.

Armhole Shaping

Beg Chart 3, keeping in alignment with Chart 2 (see arrows) and BO 9 sts at marker at beg of ea Armhole edge—108 (126, 144) sts on ea side. Change to size 5 straight needles, placing sts for Front on holder, and work Front separately from Back.

Back Neck

When 10 rows of chart rem, beg Neckline shaping.

NEXT ROW (RS): BO center 18 (20, 20) sts, attaching separate balls of yarn to work both sides at the same time.

BO 9 sts at Neck edge on next 2 rows, then BO 4 sts at Neck edge on next 2 rows—64 (80, 98) sts on ea side of Neck. AT THE SAME TIME, beg Shoulder shaping.

Shoulder Shaping

SIZE 36: Beg binding off for Shoulder when 8 rows of chart rem. At Armhole edge, BO 8 sts at beg of row 4 times.

SIZE 42: Beg binding off for Shoulder when 6 rows of chart rem. At Armhole edge, BO 13 sts at beg of row 2 times, then 14 sts once.

SIZE 48: Work even to top of chart. BO all sts.

Front

Work same as for Back until 20 rows of Chart 3 rem, then beg Neckline shaping.

NEXT ROW (RS): BO center 24 (26, 26) sts, joining separate balls of yarn to work both sides at the same time.

BO 6 sts at Neck edge on next 2 rows, then BO 1 st at ea Neck edge 4 times—64 (80, 98) sts on ea side of Neck. Work even to top of chart, working Shoulder shaping same as for Back.

Sleeves

Using size 4 needles and CC5 CO 54 (57, 66) sts.

Join CC1, and work in Corrugated Rib for 4 rows. Cut yarns.

Join MC and CC3 and work 6 rows of Sleeve Chart 1, inc 3 sts evenly spaced across first row—57 (60, 69) sts.

Change to size 5 needles and work 2 rows in MC, inc 3 (6, 3) sts evenly spaced along the first row—60 (66, 72) sts. AT THE SAME TIME, foll chart sequence shaping the Sleeve as foll:

Sleeve Shaping

Work one row of Sleeve Chart 1 to set up the pattern. Thereafter, and AT THE SAME TIME FOLLOWING CHART SEQUENCE, inc 1 st ea end of row every RS row until there are 114 (118, 120) sts. Thereafter inc every 4th row until there are 132 (138, 144) sts. Then work even as foll:

Chart Sequence

Work Sleeve Chart 1, then work 2 rows in MC.

Work Sleeve Chart 1 3 (3, 4) times with ea rep foll by 1 row in MC.

Then work 4 reps of Sleeve Chart 1 with no plain rows between ea rep.

Work a 5th rep of the same chart, but work the Transition Row on Sleeve Chart 2 as the final row.

Cont with Sleeve Chart 2 until Sleeve meas 21½ (23½, 23½)" (55 [60, 60]cm). Work one plain row in MC, then foll Sleeve Chart 3. BO all sts.

Finishing

Weave in ends. Sew one Shoulder seam. Using size 4 needles and MC on RS pick up and k 44 (46, 46) sts along Back Neck edge, 9 sts along ea straight side of Front Neck, and 44 (46, 46) sts along Front—106 (110, 110) sts.

Join CC3 and work 4 rows of Chart 1. Cut yarns.

Join CC1 and CC5 and work in Corrugated Rib for 2 rows then cut CC1. BO using CC5.

Sew rem Shoulder and Neck seam. Set Sleeves into Armholes, then sew Sleeve seams. A narrow elastic can be worked into Sleeve ends if needed. Weave in remaining ends.

Note: Read charts from bottom up, and right to left on all Right Side rounds or rows, and from left to right on Wrong Side rows. Strand the unused color across the Wrong Side, taking care to not work too tightly.

FOREST CHART KEY

■ MC

■ CC1

+ CC2

• CC3

○ CC4

□ CC5

— CC6

△ CC7

CHART 1

CHART 2   CHART 3

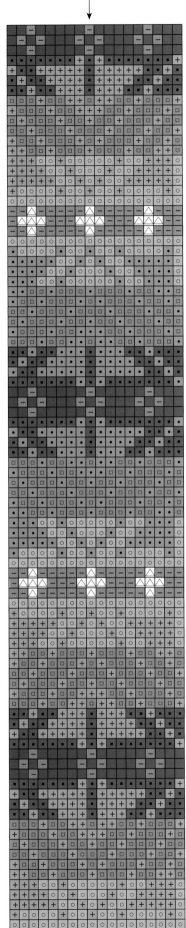

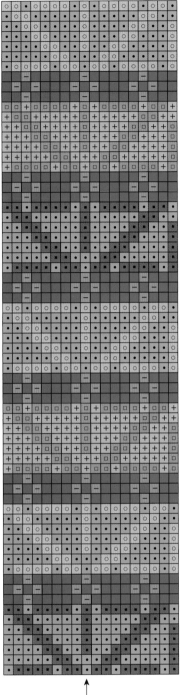

← BEGIN BACK NECK SHAPING HERE

← BEGIN FRONT NECK SHAPING HERE

SLEEVE CHART 1

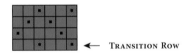

SLEEVE CHART 2

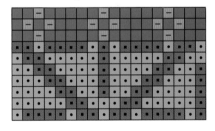

← TRANSITION ROW

SLEEVE CHART 3

↑
KEEP IN ALIGNMENT WITH CHART 2

DEW ON LILAC

Beads sparkle like drops of dew on a tunic edged and collared in nostalgic "Old Shale" lace. The yarn in this sweater is a blend of rayon and cotton in which the rayon takes center stage, creating a sleek appearance. A small amount of machine sewing is required to complete this sweater, but the elegant look is well worth the effort. A set of interchangeable circular needles can come in handy when knitting the lace collar, but aren't required.

SKILL LEVEL
Intermediate

METHOD
Knit

SIZES
To fit actual bust/hip size: 31½/33½ (34/36½, 36/38½, 39/41½, 42/44½)" (80/85 [86/93, 91/98, 99/105, 107/113]cm)

FINISHED MEASUREMENTS
Hip: Approx 36 (39¼, 41½, 44½, 47¾)" (91 [100, 105, 113, 121]cm)

Note: Due to the 18-stitch repeat of the lace pattern, shaping varies between the sizes. Make the size appropriate for your hip measurement.

YARN
14 (14, 15, 16, 17) (1¾ oz./50g, 120 yd./110m) skeins DK weight yarn

NEEDLES
Size US 3 (3.25mm) straight needles

Size US 4 (3.5mm) straight needles

47" (120cm) size US 4 (3.5mm) circular needle

47" (120cm) size US 6 (4mm) circular needle

47" (120cm) size US 8 (5mm) circular needle

47" (120cm) size US 9 (5.5mm) circular needle

If necessary, change needle size to obtain correct gauge.

NOTIONS
Yarn needle

1 yd. (1m) ⅜" (1cm) elastic

40g box of 6/0 seed beads

Dental floss threader

Tapestry needle that will fit through seed beads

Sewing machine

Pins

Thread to match yarn color

GAUGE
24 sts and 30 rows = 4" (10cm) in St st on size US 4 (3.5mm) needles

One rep of Old Shale on size US 4 (3.5mm) needles = 3¼" (8cm)

The project shown at right was made using Garnstudio Cotton Viscose (54% cotton/46% viscose, 1¾ oz./50g, 120 yd./110m) in color 27 Light Purple.

The project shown at right was made using Dyna-Mites in Ceylon Pastel Grey.

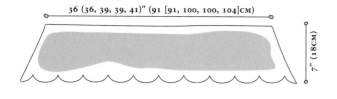

36 (36, 39, 39, 41)" (91 [91, 100, 100, 104]CM)

7" (18CM)

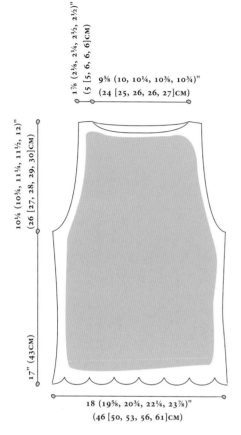

1⅞ (2⅛, 2¼, 2½, 2½)" (5 [5, 6, 6, 6]CM)

9⅝ (10, 10¼, 10⅜, 10¾)" (24 [25, 26, 26, 27]CM)

10¼ (10¾, 11¼, 11½, 12)" (26 [27, 28, 29, 30]CM)

17" (43CM)

18 (19⅝, 20¾, 22¼, 23⅞)" (46 [50, 53, 56, 61]CM)

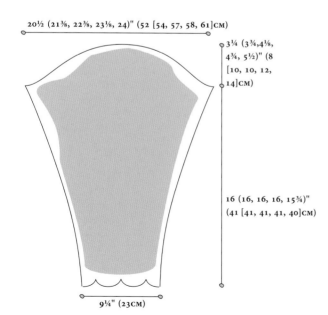

20½ (21⅜, 22⅜, 23⅛, 24)" (52 [54, 57, 58, 61]CM)

3¼ (3¾, 4⅛, 4¾, 5½)" (8 [10, 10, 12, 14]CM)

16 (16, 16, 16, 15¾)" (41 [41, 41, 41, 40]CM)

9¼" (23CM)

PATTERN STITCHES

OLD SHALE (MULT OF 18 + 1 STS)

ROW 1 (RS): *K1, [k2tog] 3 times, [yo, k1] 5 times, yo, [k2tog] 3 times; rep from * to last st, k1.

ROW 2: K all sts.

ROW 3: K all sts.

ROW 4: P all sts.

Rep Rows 1–4 for patt.

Back

Using size 4 needles, CO 109 (127, 127, 145, 145) sts. Work 6 reps of Old Shale patt.

NEXT ROW (RS): Work Row 1 of Old Shale patt.

NEXT ROW (WS): K2tog, p rem sts.

Change to size 3 needles. Cont in St st and dec 1 st ea end of row every 8 rows 0 (5, 1, 6, 1) times—108 (116, 124, 132, 142) sts. Work even until piece meas 17" (43cm).

Armhole Shaping

BO 3 sts at beg of next 2 rows—102 (110, 118, 126, 136) sts.

BO 2 sts at beg of next 2 rows 1 (1, 1, 2, 3) times—98 (106, 114, 118, 124) sts.

BO 1 st ea end of row every RS row 2 (4, 5, 6, 8) times—94 (98, 104, 106, 108) sts.

BO 1 st ea end of row every 4th row 6 (6, 7, 7, 6) times—82 (86, 90, 92, 96) sts.

Work even until Armhole meas 9½ (10, 10½, 10¾, 11¼)" (24 [25, 27, 27, 29]cm).

Back Neck

Work 22 (23, 24, 25, 26) sts, join a second ball of yarn and BO center 38 (40, 42, 42, 44) sts, work even to end.

Working both sides at once, BO 9 sts at ea Neck edge once, then 1 st twice. Work even until Armhole meas 10¼ (10¾, 11¼, 11½, 12)" (26 [27, 29, 29, 30]cm).

BO rem 11 (12, 13, 14, 15) sts on ea Shoulder.

Front

Work same as for Back until Armhole meas 8 (8, 8½, 8¾, 9)" (20 [20, 22, 22, 23]cm).

Front Neck

Work 31 (32, 33, 34, 35) sts, join a second ball of yarn and BO center 20 (22, 24, 24, 26) sts, work even to end.

Working both sides at once, BO 6 sts at ea Neck edge, then 4 sts, then 2 sts, then BO 1 st at ea Neck edge every row 8 times.

Work even until Armhole meas 10¼ (10¾, 11¼, 11½, 12)" (26 [27, 29, 29, 30]cm).

BO rem 11 (12, 13, 14, 15) sts on ea Shoulder.

Sleeves

Using size 4 needles, CO 55 sts. Work 6 reps of Old Shale patt.

NEXT ROW (RS): Work Row 1 of Old Shale patt.

NEXT ROW (WS): P, inc 1 (1, 5, 5, 7) sts evenly spaced across row.

Change to size 3 needles. Cont in St st and inc 1 st ea end of row every 4th row until there are 94 (96, 100, 96, 92) sts. Work even until piece meas 14¾ (14, 14, 13, 11½)" (37 [36, 36, 33, 29]cm).

Inc 1 st ea end of every RS row until there are 122 (128, 134, 138, 144) sts. Work even until piece meas 16 (16, 16, 16, 15¾)" (41 [41, 41, 41, 40]cm).

Sleeve Cap

BO 7 sts at beg of next 2 rows—108 (114, 120, 124, 130) sts.

BO 6 sts at beg of next 2 rows—96 (102, 108, 112, 118) sts.

BO 3 sts at beg of next 2 rows 3 (2, 2, 1, 1) times—78 (90, 96, 106, 112) sts.

BO 2 sts at beg of next 2 rows 5 (10, 10, 14, 18) times—58 (50, 56, 50, 40) sts.

BO 3 sts at beg of next 2 (0, 2, 2, 0) rows—52 (50, 50, 44, 40) sts.

BO 4 sts at beg of next 2 (2, 2, 0, 0) rows—44 (42, 42, 44, 40) sts.

BO 6 sts at beg of next 2 rows.

BO rem 32 (30, 30, 32, 28) sts.

Cowl Collar

Check that several yards (meters) of yarn at the beg of the skein are free of knots. Place a dental floss threader on the end of the yarn and string 198 (198, 216, 216, 234) beads onto the yarn.

Note: To knit the Collar, use circular needles to accommodate the large number of sts, and work back and forth (do not join into a rnd).

Using size 9 circular needles, CO 199 (199, 217, 217, 235) sts, adding a bead with ea cast-on st.

Work 3 reps of Old Shale patt. Change to size 8 circular needle and work 3 reps of Old Shale patt. Change to size 6 circular needle and work 3 reps of Old Shale patt. Finally, change to size 4 circular needle and work 3 reps of Old Shale patt.

Work Row 1 of Old Shale patt once more, then p 1 row. BO.

Finishing

Weave in all ends, weaving ends back and forth to secure them. Block ea piece. Sew Shoulder seams. Lay sweater on a flat surface. Meas the elastic by laying it around the Neck edge, then cut elastic 3" (8cm) shorter than Neck edge circumference. Overlap elastic ends and sew together. Divide elastic evenly into fourths using sewing pins to mark the sections. Do the same with the sweater Neckline. Pin the elastic to the inside of the sweater Neckline, matching the pins and having the elastic ⅛" (3mm) lower than Neckline. Using an average stitch length and straight stitch, and while keeping the elastic stretched to fit the Neckline, machine sew the upper edge of elastic to the upper edge of sweater. Keeping elastic stretched as before, sew a second line of stitching along lower edge of elastic.

Set Sleeves into Armholes and sew Sleeve and side seams.

Pin the Collar to Neckline, beg and ending at center Back and distributing evenly around Neck. The Collar is longer than Neckline—gather it while sewing. Then, after Collar is sewn on, using yarn and yarn needle, loosely sew through all layers along center of elastic making a simple running stitch with sts about ⅜" (1cm) long. This keeps the edge from rolling. Back seam of Collar remains open.

Randomly sew seed beads in a scattered fashion onto Front of sweater. Sew on beads one at a time using the same yarn, or use beading thread. Weave in remaining ends.

VIOLET HEATHER

The hem of this skirt is both rounded and lightly flared, which will make it ripple gracefully as you walk. Linen makes a beautiful skirt and the weight of this yarn keeps the garment light and airy. The skirt is knitted from the top down in six sections, is finished with a folded hem, and features crocheted vertical seaming for a slimming effect. Alternatively, seams can be hand sewn, although this eliminates the linear effect.

SKILL LEVEL
Beginner

METHOD
Knit and Crochet

SIZES
To fit actual hip size: 35½ (37½, 40, 43, 46)" (90 [95, 102, 109, 117]cm)

Note: Skirt fits at the top of the hip, below waist.

FINISHED MEASUREMENTS
Hip: Approx 39½ (42, 44½, 48, 50½)" (100 [107, 113, 122, 128]cm)

YARN
7 (8, 9, 10, 10) (1¾ oz./50g, 130 yd./119m) skeins DK weight yarn

NEEDLES
Size US 4 (3.5mm) straight needles

32" (80cm) size US 4 (3.5mm) circular needle

If necessary, change needle size to obtain correct gauge.

HOOK
Size US D/3 (3.25mm) crochet hook

NOTIONS
Yarn needle

Large safety pin

1 (1, 1, 1, 1⅛) yd. (1 [1, 1, 1, 1.1]m) 1" (3cm) elastic

GAUGE
20 sts and 26 rows = 4" (10cm) in St st on size US 4 (3.5mm) needles

The project shown at right was made using Garnstudio Drops Lin (100% linen, 1¾ oz./50g, 130 yd./119m) in color 106.

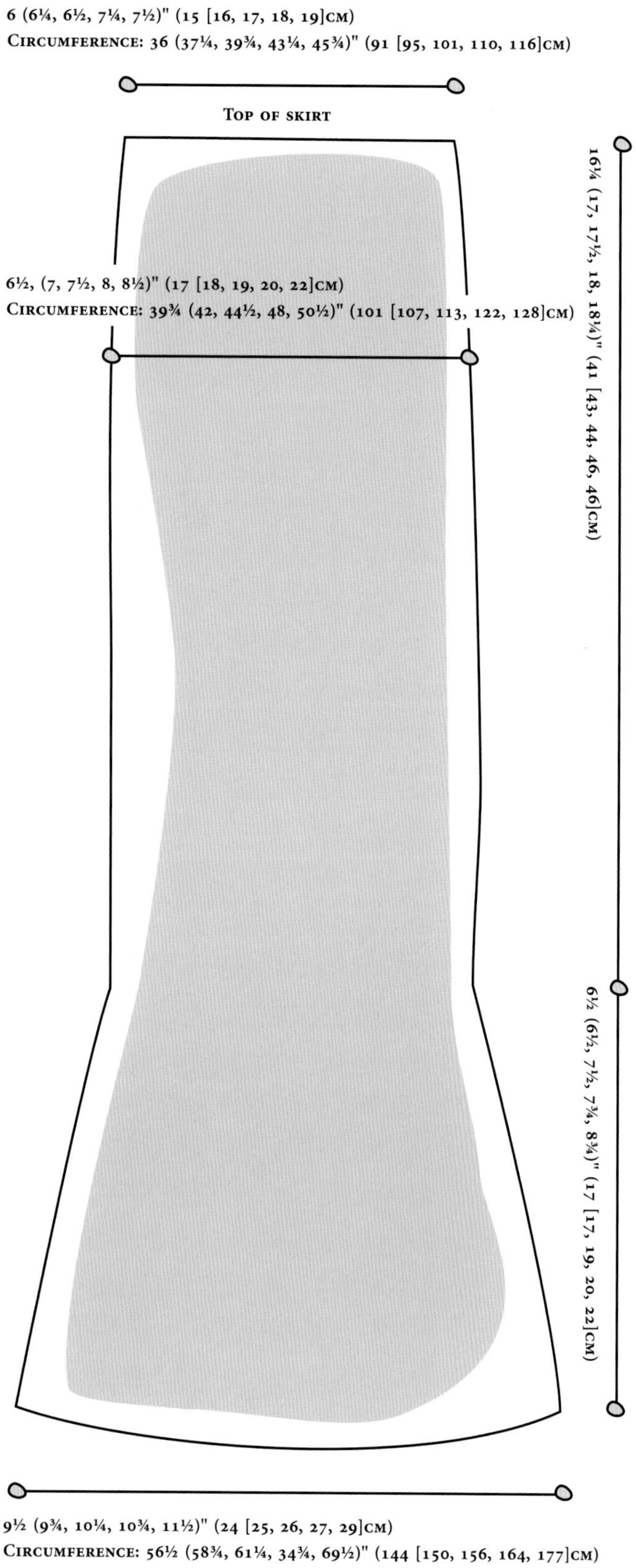
6 (6¼, 6½, 7¼, 7½)" (15 [16, 17, 18, 19]cm)
Circumference: 36 (37¼, 39¾, 43¼, 45¾)" (91 [95, 101, 110, 116]cm)
Top of skirt
6½, (7, 7½, 8, 8½)" (17 [18, 19, 20, 22]cm)
Circumference: 39¾ (42, 44½, 48, 50½)" (101 [107, 113, 122, 128]cm)
16¼ (17, 17½, 18, 18¼)" (41 [43, 44, 46, 46]cm)
6½ (6½, 7½, 7¾, 8¾)" (17 [17, 19, 20, 22]cm)
9½ (9¾, 10¼, 10¾, 11½)" (24 [25, 26, 27, 29]cm)
Circumference: 56½ (58¾, 61¼, 34¾, 69½)" (144 [150, 156, 164, 177]cm)

ABBREVIATIONS

INCRH
Inc 1 st on the right-hand edge of RS.

INCLH
Inc 1 st on the left-hand edge of RS.

Skirt Section (make 6)

Note: The skirt is knitted from the top down, making it easy to fit in case you want to change the length. Make any length adjustment before knitting the flare.

Increases are staggered to keep a smooth seam.

Using size 4 straight needles and beg at the top of the skirt, CO 30 (31, 33, 36, 38) sts. Work in St st, inc as foll:

At ½ (½, ⅝, 1, 1¼)" (1 [1, 2, 3, 3]cm): IncRH 1 st.

At 1½ (⅝, ¾, 1¼, 1⅜)" (4 [2, 2, 3, 4]cm): IncLH 1 st.

At 2⅝ (2½, 2, 5⅛, 6)" (6 [6, 5, 13, 15]cm): IncRH 1 st.

At – (3½, 4, 6, 9½)" (– [9, 10, 15, 24]cm): IncLH 1 st—33 (35, 37, 40, 42) sts.

Work even until piece meas 16¼ (17, 17½, 18, 18¼)" (41 [43, 44, 46, 47]cm) from beg.

Skirt Flare

NEXT ROW: IncRH 1 st, and IncLH 1 st 2 rows later. Rep these incs at 1" (3cm) intervals beg 1" (3cm) from the first inc 6 (6, 6, 6, 7) times more; 14 (14, 14, 14, 16) sts inc—47 (49, 51, 54, 58) sts.

Work even until skirt meas 22¾ (23½, 25, 25¾, 27)" (58 [60, 64, 65, 69]cm) from beg.

Rounded Hem

Dec at beg of next 2 rows: 2 sts, then 3 sts, then 4 sts, then 6 sts, then BO all sts.

Finishing

Weave in ends. Block ea piece. For ea Skirt Section, fold under the lower edge evenly ⅝" (2cm) and lightly steam press. Using yarn and yarn needle, lightly sew the hems, taking care that stitching does not show on the RS.

Place 2 sections with WS tog and pin along side seam (or baste about ½" [1cm] away from the edge). Using crochet hook, join yarn at bottom edge and sl st the seam closed from bottom to top, working into one thread of ea Skirt Section and taking care that the seam lies smoothly with no puckering or stretching. Fasten off at top and rep until all sections are seamed.

Using size 4 circular needles, pick up and k 30 (31, 33, 36, 38) sts along top of ea section—180 (186, 198, 216, 228) sts. Work in the rnd in St st for 1⅛" (3cm). P 1 rnd, then cont to k every rnd until waistband meas 2¼" (6cm). BO.

Fold waistband to inside along the p rnd, and sew to top of skirt leaving an opening. Place a large safety pin on one end of the elastic and thread it through the band. Overlap ends and pin. Try on skirt, adjusting elastic until it fits comfortably. Sew elastic tog and trim excess. Finish sewing the waistband. Weave in remaining ends.

ADDING A ZIPPER

Elastic waistbands are easy to make and to wear, but if you prefer a more fitted look, shape the top of the skirt and put in a zipper. Using your body circumference where the skirt is to fit (allowing 1" (3cm) for the waistband to be added later), multiply your measurement by the stitch gauge, then divide by 6 and use this number of stitches to begin each panel of the skirt. Work steady and smooth increases on each side edge (stagger them as described in the pattern) until the number of stitches is the same as at approximately 3–4" (8–10cm) of the pattern. Then follow the pattern to the end. Work the waistband in rows instead of rounds, and leave one skirt seam partially open for the zipper. Insert a 7" (18cm) zipper.

BLOOMIN' LILAC

This lace-knitted and beaded linen belt can be a lovely accessory for any outfit. Choose yarn and beads to create your own custom look.

SKILL LEVEL
Advanced Beginner

Knitting with beads is not difficult, but requires patience.

METHOD
Knit and Crochet

FINISHED MEASUREMENTS
Approx 2½" (6cm) wide × desired length

YARN
2 (1¾ oz./50g, 130 yd./119m) skeins DK weight yarn

NEEDLES
Size US 4 (3.5mm) straight needles

If necessary, change needle size to obtain correct gauge.

HOOK
Size US F/5 (3.75mm) crochet hook

NOTIONS
Yarn needle

2" (5cm) wide belt buckle without prong

40g box of 6/0 seed beads

Dental floss threader

GAUGE
Lace Panel is 2¼" (6cm) wide

The project shown at right was made using Garnstudio Drops Lin (100% linen, 1¾ oz./50g, 130 yd./119m) in color 106.

The project shown at right was made using Dyna-Mites in Transparent Matte Lilac.

PATTERN STITCHES

LACE PANEL (WORKED OVER CENTER 9 STS)

ROW 1 (RS): K4, yo, SKP, k3.

ROW 2 (AND ALL WS ROWS THROUGH 12): P all sts.

ROW 3: K2, k2tog, yo, k1, yo, SKP, k2.

ROW 5: K1, k2tog, yo, k3, yo, SKP, k1.

ROW 7: K2tog, yo, k5, yo, SKP.

ROWS 9 AND 11: P, sliding a bead up to ea st over center 9 sts (do not bead end sts).

Rep Rows 1–12 for patt.

Belt

Note: Yarn is used doubled throughout, with the beads on one strand only. As a precaution, hand-wind one skein to check that there are no knots to interfere with the beads. Using the dental floss threader, string all of the seed beads onto the hand-wound skein of yarn. Move the beads along as you knit.

Using size 4 needles with one strand of the beaded yarn and one of the plain yarn held tog, CO 11 sts.

Note: For a neat edge, slip the first and last st on every RS row throughout; p these sts on the WS.

Work in St st for 2" (5cm).

NEXT ROW (RS): Change to Lace patt, working patt on central 9 sts, and slipping end sts on RS and purling these on WS.

Work to the length desired—the 2" (5cm) St st section at beg will be folded 1" (3cm) to the back, so the end of the lace-knit section should meet with this fold. Change to St st and work for 3" (8cm), ending with a WS row.

NEXT ROW (RS): Sl1, k2tog, work in St st to last 3 sts, k2tog, sl1.

NEXT ROW (WS): P all sts.

Rep these 2 rows until 5 sts rem. BO all sts. Keep beads on the rem yarn.

Finishing

Using crochet hook and working on the WS with doubled yarn, join yarn at the buckle end. Sl st in ea st along edge to the beg of the patt st section. Change to sc, sliding a bead up to ea st as it is worked.

Work beaded sc to the belt-tip end where patt ends and St st begs. Change to unbeaded sl st as before and work around the tip, reverting again to beaded sc along Lace section on opposite side of Belt. Change again to unbeaded sl st at the buckle end. Fasten off.

Fold 1" (3cm) of buckle end over the center bar of the buckle and stitch to the WS of the Belt. Lightly steam press Belt on WS.

Weave in ends.

SILVER SAXIFRAGE

Crocheted worsted weight hemp makes a sturdy belt. Take your time crocheting with worsted weight hemp; it will feel firm and coarse, but it will create a long-lasting accessory. I dressed up this functional belt with a lovely silver buckle.

SKILL LEVEL	FINISHED MEASUREMENTS	YARN	HOOK	NOTIONS	GAUGE
Intermediate	Approx 4" (10cm) wide × desired length	1 (17½ oz./500g, 425 yd./389m) cone worsted weight yarn	Size US F/5 (3.75mm) crochet hook	Yarn needle	20 sc = 4" (10cm)
METHOD				Screwdriver	
Crochet			*If necessary, change hook size to obtain correct gauge.*	1½" (4cm) wide belt buckle with prong, metal keeper and belt end	

The project shown at right was made using Lanaknits Hemp12 (100% hemp, 17½ oz./500g, 425 yd./389m) in color Natural. This project only uses a small amount of the yarn on the cone. I suggest using the remaining yarn to create a matching purse, such as Wild Oats on page 120.

The project shown at right was made using a buckle set from Tandy Leather Factory.

Belt

Using size F/5 crochet hook, ch 7, then ch 1 more and turn.

ROW 1: Sc in ea ch across—7 sc. Ch 1 to turn.

Rep Row 1 until piece meas 2½" (6cm). Ch 1 to turn.

NEXT ROW: [Sc in sc] 3 times, ch 1, skip 1 to make a hole for the buckle prong, [sc in sc] 3 times. Ch 1 to turn.

NEXT ROW: [Sc in sc] 3 times, sc into space made by ch-1 on prev row, [sc in sc] 3 times.

Cont to work even in sc until piece meas 5" (13cm).

NEXT ROW: Turn, ch 2 (counts as 1 dc), 3 dc into first st (4-dc shell made), [skip 2 sc, 4-dc shell in next sc] twice. Ch 1 to turn.

NEXT ROW: Sl st into first 2 dc, then sl st between 2nd and 3rd dc of shell. Ch 2 (counts as 1 dc), 5 dc into same place (6-dc shell made), [6-dc shell into center of next 4-dc shell] twice. Ch 1 to turn.

NEXT ROW: Sl st into first 2 dc, then sl st into center of 6-dc shell, and cont as prev row making 6-dc shell over shell on every row until Belt is desired length. Ch 1 to turn.

NEXT ROW: Sl st to center of shell. Make a 4-dc shell on top of ea shell across row. Ch 1, turn. Sc, dec 5 sts across row. Ch 1, turn. Work in sc on 7 sts making a prong hole every 1" (3cm) as described earlier, until prong hole end is 5" (13cm). Work one fewer st ea row until 4 sts rem. Fasten off.

Finishing

Place metal keeper and buckle onto buckle end of Belt, inserting prong through prong hole. Fold end to back and stitch through all layers both before and after the keeper. Force metal end onto opposite end of Belt (use a flat screwdriver) and screw in the two screws, making sure the screws push into the fabric. Weave in ends.

CHOCOLATE DUST

This capelet made of bamboo takes on the color of the dusty coating of cocoa powder on truffles. Bamboo is soft and silky and lends an air of sophistication to any project. The ribbed band on this capelet can be worn to the front, back or on the left shoulder.

SKILL LEVEL
Experienced

METHOD
Knit and Crochet

SIZE
One size

FINISHED MEASUREMENTS
Approx 56" (142cm) around lower edge

YARN
9 (1¾ oz./50g, 112 yd./102m) skeins sport weight yarn

NEEDLES
Size US 1 (2.25mm) straight needles

Size US 4 (3.5mm) straight needles

40" (100cm) or 47" (120cm) size US 4 (3.5mm) circular needles

If necessary, change needle size to obtain correct gauge.

HOOK
US Size 00 (3.5mm) steel crochet hook

NOTIONS
Cable needle

Yarn needle

6 crystal ball buttons, ⅜" (1cm) diameter

GAUGE
24 sts and 32 rows = 4" (10cm) in St st on size US 4 (3.5mm) needles

Cable & Bobble Panel = 5" (13cm) wide

5 reps of the Cable & Bobble Panel = 15½" (39cm)

The project shown at right was made using Rowan Classic Bamboo Soft (100% bamboo, 1¾ oz./50g, 112 yd./102m) in color 106 Beaver.

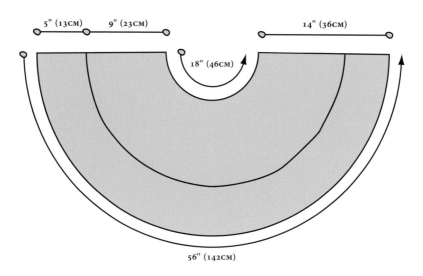

5" (13CM) 9" (23CM) 14" (36CM)

18" (46CM)

56" (142CM)

ABBREVIATIONS

B
Bobble.

C4B
Slip 2 sts to cn and hold to back, k2, k2 from cn.

C6B
Slip 3 sts to cn and hold to back, k3, k3 from cn.

C6F
Slip 3 sts to cn and hold to front, k3, k3 from cn.

T5F
Slip 3 sts to cn and hold to front, p2, k3 from cn.

T5B
Slip 2 sts to cn and hold to back, k3, p2 from cn.

INCP
K into back, then p into front of a p st.

PATTERN STITCHES

1X1 RIB (MULT OF 2 STS)
ROW 1: *K1, p1; rep from * across.

Rep Row 1 for patt.

BOBBLE
K1, p1, k1, p1 into front of st, turn and p4, turn and k4, turn and p4, turn, sl2, k2tog, [psso] twice.

Cape Shoulders

Using size 4 circular needle, CO 107 sts.

ROW 1: [P1, k4] across, end p1.

ROW 2 AND ALL WS ROWS: K the p and p the k sts of the prev row.

ROW 3: [P1, C4B] across, end p1.

Cont as est, cabling on every 4th row, and making incs at specified intervals. Work even as est between inc rows.

AT 1" (3CM) (RS): P1, *k4 or C4B, incP; rep from * across, end p1. (There will be p2 between all cables.)

AT 1½" (4CM) (RS): P1, *k4 or C4B, incP, p1; rep from * across, end p1. (There will be p3 between all cables.)

AT 2" (5CM) (RS): P1, *k4 or C4B, incP, p2; rep from * across, end p1. (There will be p4 between all cables.)

AT 2½" (6CM) (RS): P1, *k4 or C4B, incP, p3; rep from * across, end p1. (There will be p5 between all cables.)

AT 3" (8CM) (RS): P1, *k4 or C4B, incP, p4; rep from * across, end p1. (There will be p6 between all cables.)

NEXT ROW (WS): In ea p6 section, work (k1, p4, k1). This will beg a new cable between existing cables—work the new cable on the same row as the est cable. (There will be p1 between all cables.)

AT 3½" (9CM) (RS): P1, *k4 or C4B, p1, k4 or C4B, IncP, p1; rep from * across, end p1. (P1 will alternate with p2 across row.)

AT 4" (10CM) (RS): P1, *k4 or C4B, IncP, p1, k4 or C4B, p2; rep from * across, end p1. (There will be p2 between all cables.)

AT 5" (13CM) (RS): In a non-cabling row: P1, *inc 1, k3, p2, k4, p2; rep from * across, end p1. (Every other cable will be inc to 5 sts. From here on cable these on every 6th row cabling the k4 cables on every 4th row as est. To cable 5 sts, put 2 sts on cn and hold to back, k3, k2 from cn.)

AT 6" (15CM) (RS): In a non-cabling row: P1, *inc 1, k5, p2, k4, p2; rep from * across, end p1. (Every other cable is 6 sts—keeping in pattern, C6B on every 6th row, while cabling the 4 st cables on every 4th row as est.)

AT 7" (18CM) (RS): P1, *work cable sts, IncP, p1; rep from * across, end p1. (There will be p2 between all cables.)

Work in patt as est until piece meas 9" (23cm). BO.

Cable and Bobble Panel

Using size 4 straight needles, CO 42 sts.

SET-UP ROW (WS): P3, k1, p6, k3, p6, k4, p6, k3, p6, k1, p3.

ROW 1 (RS): K1, B, k1, p1, C6F, p3, C6F, p4, C6F, p3, C6F, p1, k1, B, k1.

ROW 2 (AND ALL WS ROWS): K the p, and p the k and B sts of prev row.

ROW 3: K3, p1, k6, p3, k6, p4, k6, p3, k6, p1, k3.

ROWS 5–6: Rep Rows 1–2.

ROW 7: K3, p1, k6, p1, [T5B, T5F] twice, p1, k6, p1, k3.

ROW 9: K1, B, k1, p1, C6F, p1, k3, p4, C6F, p4, k3, p1, C6F, p1, k1, B, k1.

ROW 11: K3, p1, k6, p1, k3, p4, k6, p4, k3, p1, k6, p1, k3.

ROWS 13-22: Rep Rows 9–12 twice, then Rep Rows 9–10.

ROW 23: K3, p1, k6, p1, [T5F, T5B] twice, p1, k6, p1, k3.

Rep Rows 1–24 eighteen times, BO after Row 6.

Finishing

Weave in ends. Sew Cable & Bobble Panel to bottom of Cape Shoulders. Using size 1 needles and with RS facing, pick up and k 107 sts around neck edge.

ROW 1 (WS): P, dec 9 sts evenly spaced across row.

ROW 2: Dec 1 st at ea end of row, work 1 × 1 Rib across row. Cont in Rib, dec 1 st at ea end of every RS row. When Rib meas ¾" (2cm), BO in patt.

Left Front Underlap

With RS facing and size 1 needles, pick up and k 48 sts along Cape Shoulders section including 4 sts along end of neck ribbing, and 26 sts along end of Cable and Bobble Panel. Work in 1×1 Rib for ¾" (2cm), then BO all sts in patt. Sew on buttons placing them on the pick up and k row with the first and last button ¾" (2cm) in from the edges, and the rem ones evenly spaced between.

Right Front Overlap

With RS facing and size 1 needles, pick up and k 26 sts along end of Cable and Bobble Panel, and 48 sts along Cape Shoulders section including 4 along end of neck ribbing. Work in 1×1 Rib for 1¾" (4cm), then BO 2 sts opposite ea button for buttonholes. On foll row CO 2 sts over ea gap. When ribbing meas 2" (5cm), BO in patt. Using size 00 crochet hook, beg at the center back and work a rnd of sc around the entire cape, working (2 sc, ch 1, 2 sc) in ea corner. Fasten off. Weave in remaining ends.

SECURING BUTTONHOLES

In an inelastic knitted fabric, it is sometimes necessary to go back and sew the buttonholes to the right size. Use the sweater yarn or exactly matching thread and overcast the edges, or sew around until the hole just fits the button, then fasten off and work the ends in. This also prevents the hole from enlarging due to normal wear.

AUTUMN MAPLE

If you love to dance, this sweater is for you—the waistline does not lift when you raise your arms. Dolman sleeves add a graceful curve down to the fitted waist, and a flared and shaped peplum adds pizzazz. The sleeves are belled, and the sweater is knitted from the top down for an easy fit.

SKILL LEVEL
Beginner

METHOD
Knit and Crochet

SIZES
To fit actual bust/waist size: 31½/24 (34/26, 36/28, 39/31, 42/34)" (80/61 [86/66, 91/71, 99/79, 107/86]cm)

FINISHED MEASUREMENTS
Waist: Approx 28¾ (32, 33½, 37, 40½)" (73 [81, 85, 94, 103]cm)

YARN
15 (15, 16, 17, 18) (1¾ oz./50g, 77 yd./70m) skeins worsted weight yarn

NEEDLES
Size US 6 (4mm) straight needles (optional)

40" (100cm) size US 6 (4mm) circular needle

If necessary, change needle size to obtain correct gauge.

HOOK
Size US F/5 (3.75mm) crochet hook

NOTIONS
Yarn needle

12 buttons, ⅜" (1cm) diameter

Stitch holder

GAUGE
19 sts and 30 rows = 4" (10cm) in patt on size US 6 (4mm) needles

Note: Row gauge is very important in this project.

The project shown at right was made using Berroco Bonsai (97% bamboo/3% nylon, 1¾ oz./50g, 77 yd./70m) in color 4155 Akane Red.

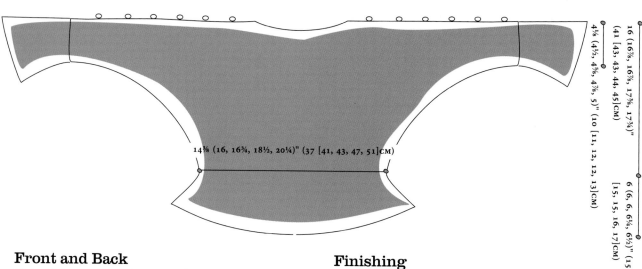

Front and Back

Note: Make two pieces the same—front and back are identical. This sweater is knit from the top down. Because of the wide cast-on edge, this sweater needs to be started on a circular needle, but if you prefer you can change to straight needles when the piece narrows sufficiently

Using 40" (102cm) circular needle CO 206 (214, 220, 228, 234) sts. Work back and forth in St st for 4⅛ (4½, 4⅝, 4⅞, 5)" (10 [11, 12, 13, 13]cm).

At beg of ea of next 2 rows BO:

6 sts, 6 sts, 4 sts, 4 sts, 3 sts, 2 sts, 3 sts, 2 sts, 3 sts, 2 sts, 2 sts, 2 sts, 1 st, 2 sts, 1 st, 2 sts, 1 st, 2 sts—106 (114, 120, 128, 134) sts.

Dec 1 st ea end of every other row 12 times—82 (90, 96, 104, 110) sts.

Dec 1 st ea end of every 4th row until 68 (76, 80, 88, 96) sts rem.

Work even until piece meas 16 (16⅞, 16⅞, 17⅜, 17¾)" (41 [43, 43, 44, 45]cm). This is the waistline, and you may want to fit the sweater before proceeding.

Put stitches on holder and set aside. Knit the second Front/Back piece to this point as well, then foll Finishing instructions for the upper edge to finish the neckline and sew the upper sleeves as stated. Baste the seams under the sleeve to the waist and try on. Adjust the waist by adding extra rows if needed, then knit the rest of the sweater.

Peplum

Inc 1 st ea end of every RS row 12 (12, 12, 13, 14) times—92 (100, 104, 114, 124) sts.

Shirttail

BO 3 sts at beg of next 2 rows 6 times—56 (64, 68, 78, 88) sts.

BO 6 sts at beg of next 2 rows 3 (3, 3, 4, 5) times.

BO rem 20 (28, 32, 30, 28) sts.

Finishing

Weave in ends. Block pieces. Place Front and Back pieces with WS tog and pin at intervals along the upper edge. Find the neck opening area: mark off center 11" (28cm), pin the ends, and try it on over your head to be sure the opening is sufficient. Sew 4" (10cm) at ea side of neck opening for shoulder.

Note: The yarn for this sweater does not work well for sewing it together. Instead, use an exactly matching doubled sewing thread or pearl cotton or any fine, smooth yarn and a tapestry needle or fine yarn needle.

Using size F/5 crochet hook, work sl st crochet along top of ea sleeve section working between shoulder and ends of sleeves.

Sew a 1" (3cm) seam at ea sleeve end (joining the sl st crochet edges). Divide the area between shoulder and sleeve end equally and place 6 pins so there are 7 open sections and sew together at ea pin, sewing on a button at the same time.

To form neckline, fold in 1" (3cm) at center of neck opening on Front and Back sections, tapering to nothing at ea shoulder. Loosely sew in place.

Sleeve Cuffs

At sleeve ends and with RS facing, pick up and k 16 (18, 19, 20, 20) sts across ea of Front and Back sections—32 (36, 38, 40, 40) sts.

ROW 1: P, inc 4 sts evenly spaced across row. Cont in St st and inc 1 st at ea side edge every 4th row 8 times—52 (56, 58, 60, 60) sts. Cuff should meas 5" (13cm).

BO 3 sts at beg of next 2 rows 3 times. BO rem 34 (38, 40, 42, 42) sts.

Sew underarm seams from sleeve ends to bottom of sweater.

Using size F/5 crochet hook, work sc around edges of Sleeve Cuffs and bottom edge of sweater. Weave in remaining ends.

WILD BLUEBERRY

Wild Blueberry begins as a graceful dolman sleeve which, as you knit, turns into a shawl with a kimono-style neckline. The knitted pattern consists of randomly placed holes on one half, and tabs on the other. Wrap the front ends and tie them behind your back, or let them drape. Use a shawl pin as a closure.

SKILL LEVEL
Beginner

METHOD
Knit and Crochet

SIZES
One size

FINISHED MEASUREMENTS
Approx 57" (145cm) cuff to cuff

Approx. 22" (56cm) from shoulder to bottom edge

YARN
6 (3½ oz./100g, 165 yd./151m) skeins sport weight yarn

NEEDLES
47" (120cm) size US 10 (6mm) circular needle

Size US 11 (8mm) straight needles

1 extra size US 11 (8mm) straight needle for three-needle bind off (optional)

If necessary, change needle size to obtain correct gauge.

HOOK
Size US F/5 (3.75mm) crochet hook

NOTIONS
Stitch holder

Yarn needle

GAUGE
13 sts and 20 rows = 4" (10cm) in St st on size US 10 (6mm) needles

The project shown at right was made using Lanaknits Allhemp6 (100% hemp, 3½ oz./100g, 165 yd./151m) in color 016 Deep Sea.

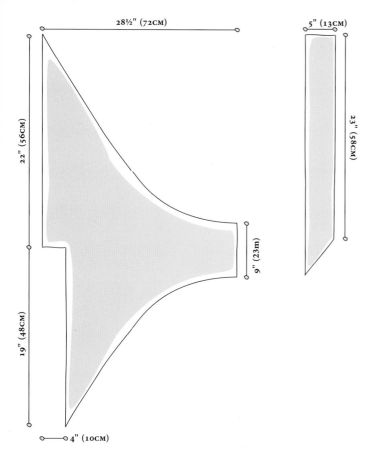

PATTERN STITCHES

HOLES

At placement for a Hole, work (yo, k2tog). Place Holes as desired. You can work as many or as few as you like. See photo at right for suggested placements.

TABS

At placement for a Tab, CO 3 sts, then BO 3 sts. Same as for the Holes, place them as desired, aiming for a number roughly equal to the Holes.

Right Sleeve

Note: Knitting begins at cuff edge of sleeve.

Using size 10 circular needles, CO 30 sts. Work even in St st for 3" (8cm), ending after a WS row.

NEXT ROW (RS): Inc 1 st at ea end of row.

Inc 1 st ea end every 4th row until there are 44 sts. Work the next 3 rows even, then inc 1 st at ea end of every RS row and, AT THE SAME TIME, beg random Holes as described above. Cont to make Holes throughout.

Cont as est until there are 126 sts, ending with a WS row.

NEXT ROW (RS): Inc 1, BO 63 sts (front), work across rem 63 sts (back), inc 1 at the end. Cont to inc on RS at lower edge as est, and work straight at neck edge until there are 73 sts. BO. (Or, if you prefer, place these sts on a holder and later work three-needle BO to attach to the Left Sleeve section.)

Piece should meas approx 28½" (72cm) from cuff of sleeve to center back.

Left Sleeve

Work same as Right Sleeve, but make Tabs instead of Holes until there are 126 sts, ending with a RS row.

NEXT ROW (WS): Inc 1, BO 63 sts (front), work across rem 63 sts (back), inc 1 at the end. Cont to inc as est on lower edge of back and work even at neck edge until there are 73 sts. BO or join to Right Sleeve section using three-needle BO.

Left Front Band

Using size 11 needles, CO 3 sts.

ROW 1 (RS): Inc in first st, k rem sts.

ROW 2 (AND ALL WS ROWS): P all sts.

Rep Rows 1–2 until there are 15 sts. AT THE SAME TIME, make Holes as described earlier. Work even until shorter edge meas 23" (58cm). Place sts on holder.

Right Front Band

Using size 11 needles, CO 3 sts.

ROW 1 (RS): K across row, inc in final st.

ROW 2 (AND ALL WS ROWS): P all sts.

Rep Rows 1–2 until there are 15 sts. AT THE SAME TIME, make Tabs as described earlier. Work even until shorter edge meas 23" (58cm). Work three-needle BO to join Left and Right Front Bands.

Finishing

Weave in ends. Block pieces.

Sew or sl st crochet the back seam on the WS with RS facing, unless it was joined by three-needle BO. Sew the shorter edge of Bands to fronts and neck edges. Sew underarm seams for 18" (46cm) in from cuffs, then fasten off.

Using size F/5 crochet hook, join yarn at bottom edge of Right Front Band. Work from the bottom of the Right Front Band around to the bottom of the Left Front Band, placing sts about ½" (1cm) apart and working into 2 loops of the knitting for ea st. Ch 5 (counts as dc, ch 3), dc in same place. *(Dc, ch 3, dc) in next space; rep from * to end. Fasten off. Rejoin into first ch-3 loop at beg of Right Front Band and work (2 sc, ch 3, 2 sc) in ch-3 loop, ch 1. Cont as est, ending (2 sc, ch 3, 2 sc). Fasten off. Work a row of sc along bottom edges of shawl, including the sloping edges of Bands. Work a rnd of sc around Sleeve cuffs. Weave in remaining ends.

GARDEN'S EVE

Knit this little bolero and embroider it with dusky evening flowers. This piece is knitted all in one with a semifitted bodice and medium-length sleeves with fold-back cuffs. Soft cotton, long-wearing hemp and drapey rayon combined make a wonderfully wearable fabric.

SKILL LEVEL
Intermediate

METHOD
Knit

SIZES
To fit actual bust size: 32 (34, 36, 39, 42, 46)" [81 (86, 91, 99, 107, 117]cm)

Note: These measurements are for a semiclose fit; go one size up for a looser fit.

FINISHED MEASUREMENTS
At bottom edge: Approx 28¾ (32, 34¼, 37½, 40¾, 44¾)" (73 [81, 87, 95, 104, 114]cm)

YARN
8 (8, 10, 10, 12, 14) (2 oz./57g, 175 yd./160m) mini cones fingering weight yarn

14 skeins 6-strand embroidery floss, 1 ea of 14 colors

NEEDLES
32" (80cm) size US 6 (4mm) circular needle

47" (120cm) or 60" (150cm) size US 4 (3.5mm) circular needle

If necessary, change needle size to obtain correct gauge.

NOTIONS
Yarn needle

Tapestry needle for embroidery (optional)

GAUGE
19 sts and 28 rows = 4" (10cm) in St st on size US 6 (4mm) needles with yarn doubled

The project shown at right was made using Halcyon Block Island Blend (35% hemp/35% cotton/30% rayon, 2 oz./57g, 175 yd./160m) in color 235 Lt Purple.

The project shown at right was made using DMC 6-strand embroidery floss in colors 3779, 3776, 3722, 720, 347, 3328, 922, 402, 976, 945, 3047, 3046, 932 and 3753.

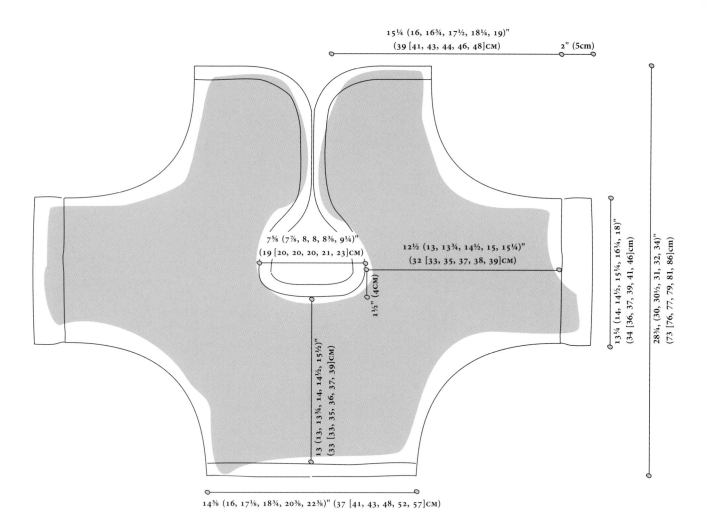

15¼ (16, 16¾, 17½, 18¼, 19)"
(39 [41, 43, 44, 46, 48]CM)

2" (5cm)

7⅝ (7⅞, 8, 8, 8⅜, 9¼)"
(19 [20, 20, 20, 21, 23]CM)

12½ (13, 13¾, 14½, 15, 15¼)"
(32 [33, 35, 37, 38, 39]CM)

1½" (4CM)

13¼ (14, 14½, 15¼, 16¼, 18)"
(34 [36, 37, 39, 41, 46]CM)

28¾ (30, 30½, 31, 32, 34)"
(73 [76, 77, 79, 81, 86]CM)

13 (13, 13¾, 14, 14½, 15½)"
(33 [33, 35, 36, 37, 39]CM)

14⅜ (16, 17⅛, 18¾, 20⅜, 22⅜)" (37 [41, 43, 48, 52, 57]CM)

Back

Note: Sweater begins at bottom of Back.

With 2 strands of yarn held tog throughout and using size 6 circular needles, CO 70 (78, 84, 90, 98, 108) sts.

Work in St st for 1½ (1½, 1¾, 1½, 1, 1¼)" (4 [4, 4, 4, 3, 3]cm).

NEXT ROW: Inc 1 st ea end of row.

Inc 1 st ea end of every 4th row 3 (3, 4, 5, 7, 7) times—78 (86, 94, 102, 114, 122) sts.

Inc 1 st ea end of every other row 7 (13, 7, 7, 3, 5) times—106 (112, 108, 116, 120, 132) sts.

Shaping is different for ea size. Inc at beg of ea of next 2 rows:

SIZE 32: 3 sts, then 3 sts, then 6 sts, then 21 sts—172 sts.

SIZE 34: 3 sts, then 3 sts, then 6 sts, then 23 sts—182 sts.

SIZE 36: 2 sts, then 2 sts, then 3 sts, then 3 sts, then 4 sts, then 26 sts—188 sts.

SIZE 39: 2 sts, then 2 sts, then 3 sts, then 3 sts, then 5 sts, then 24 sts—194 sts.

SIZE 42: [2 sts] 4 times, then 3 sts, then 5 sts, then 25 sts—202 sts.

SIZE 46: 2 sts, then 2 sts, then 3 sts, then 3 sts, then 5 sts, then 25 sts—208 sts.

At ea end, work 10 sts in garter st for the width of the sleeve. Work even until piece meas 13 (13, 13¾, 14, 14½, 15½)" (33 [33, 35, 36, 37, 39]cm).

Back Neck

Work 82 (82, 88, 90, 93, 94) sts, join a second ball of yarn and BO center 8 (18, 12, 14, 16, 20) sts. Work to end. Working both sides at the same time, BO at Neck Edge 10 (7, 9, 8, 8, 8) sts at beg of next 2 rows, then 3 (2, 3, 3, 3, 3) sts at beg of next 2 rows—69 (73, 76, 79, 82, 82) sts ea side.

Work even until piece meas 14¼ (14⅞, 15¼, 15⅝, 16, 17)" (36 [38, 39, 40, 41, 43]cm). Check that sleeve width meas

6⅝ (7, 7¼, 7⅝, 8¼, 9)" (17 [18, 18, 19, 21, 23]cm). Tie on a scrap of yarn to mark top of Shoulder.

Front Sleeve, Underarm and Bodice Side Shaping

Reverse the Back Underarm/Sleeve Shaping, dec instead of inc.

Front Neck

Work even for 1½ (1½, 1¾, 1¾, 1¾, 2)" (4 [4, 4, 4, 4, 5]cm).

Inc 1 st ea side of Neck Opening—70 (74, 77, 80, 83, 83) sts ea side.

Work 3 (3, 3, 3, 5, 3) rows, then inc 1 st ea side on foll row—71 (75, 78, 81, 84, 84) sts ea side.

Inc 1 st at beg of ea Neck Edge 3 (2, 2, 2, 1, 4) times—74 (77, 80, 83, 85, 88) sts ea side.

Inc 2 sts at ea Neck Edge 2 (2, 2, 2, 3, 3) times—78 (81, 84, 87, 91, 94) sts ea side.

Inc 1 st at ea Neck Edge 4 (5, 5, 5, 5, 4) times—82 (86, 89, 92, 96, 98) sts ea side.

Inc 1 st ea side on the foll 4th row (all sizes)—82 (87, 90, 93, 97, 99) sts ea side.

Work even on Front Edge (cont to shape Bodice Sides at the same time) until piece meas 12 (12¼, 12¾, 12¾, 13¼, 14⅛)" (30 [31, 32, 32, 34, 36]cm) from top of Shoulder.

BO 1 st at ea side of Front.

At 13 (13, 13¼, 13¼, 13¼, 14⅝)" (33 [33, 34, 34, 34, 37]cm) BO 1 st at ea side of Front. Then:

BO 1 st at beg of ea row at Front Opening 2 (3, 3, 1, 4, 3) times.

BO 2 sts at beg of ea row at Front Opening 2 (2, 2, 3, 2, 4) times.

BO 3 sts at beg of ea row at Front Opening 1 (1, 1, 0, 1, 0) times.

BO 4 sts at beg of ea row at Front Opening 0 (0, 0, 1, 0, 0) times.

BO 5 sts at beg of ea row at Front Opening 0 (0, 0, 0, 1, 1) times.

Check that Front meas the same as the Back. BO rem 21 (23, 26, 27, 28, 32) sts of ea Front Section.

Finishing

Weave in ends. Block pieces. Sew Side and Underarm seams.

Garter Stitch Edging

Using size 4 circular needle, with RS facing, pick up and k 4 sts per 1" (3cm) around entire edge of bolero. Working in garter st, dec 1 or 2 sts per row at inner curves of Neck and inc at outer curves of Fronts as needed in order to keep the edging lying flat. Work for 1" (3cm) then BO. Fold up the garter st sleeve cuffs and lightly sew in place.

Embroidery

Referring to the photo, embroider flowers randomly around the Front Edges. Mix and match the flower colors. Beg by working a chain st circle about ⅝" (2cm) across for ea flower, placing them as desired along Front Edges and onto the Back. Fill the circles with overlapped sts for flower centers. Work small (about ¼" [6mm]) Lazy Daisy sts for petals around ea chain st circle. Fill in around the flowers with chain st "leaves" in green shades, and French knots in light blue.

Weave in remaining ends.

FLAX

What could feel more comfortable than a linen camisole? Fabulous against the skin, wear this as a summer top or under a suit jacket. Pattern stitches are subtle in this yarn, adding to the luxuriousness of the linen's luster.

SKILL LEVEL
Experienced

METHOD
Knit and Crochet

SIZES
To fit actual bust size: 34 (37, 40)" (86 [94, 102]cm)

FINISHED MEASUREMENTS
Approx same as Sizes

YARN
1 (8¾ oz./250g, 825 yd./754m) cone fingering weight yarn

NEEDLES
Size US 1 (2.25mm) straight needles

If necessary, change needle size to obtain correct gauge.

HOOKS
Size US C/2 (2.75mm) crochet hook

Size US 0 (3.25mm) crochet hook

NOTIONS
Cable needle

Yarn needle

6 buttons, ¾" (2cm) diameter

10" (25cm) piece of ⅛" (3mm) elastic

Sewing needle

Pins

Thread to match yarn

GAUGE
29 sts and 40 rows = 4" (10cm) in Wide Rib on size US 1 (2.25mm) needles.

Note: Measure the gauge after washing the swatch—there is width shrinkage but no length shrinkage with this yarn.

The project shown at right was made using Valley Yarns 10/2 Linen (100% linen, 8¾ oz./250g, 825 yd./754m) in Natura.

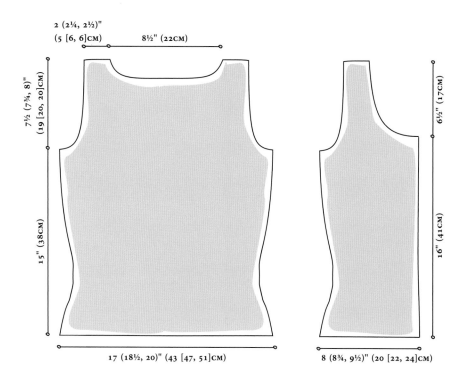

2 (2¼, 2½)"
(5 [6, 6]cm)   8½" (22cm)

7½ (7¾, 8)"
(19 [20, 20]cm)

15" (38cm)

17 (18½, 20)" (43 [47, 51]cm)

6½" (17cm)

16" (41cm)

8 (8¾, 9½)" (20 [22, 24]cm)

ABBREVIATIONS

X2R

Working in front of the first st, k the 2nd st on left-hand needle, then k the first st and drop both off needle.

X2L

Working behind the first st, k the second through the front of the stitch, then k the first st and drop both off needle.

C6B

Slip 3 sts to cn and hold to back, k3, k3 from cn.

PATTERN STITCHES

ZIGZAG (MULT OF 14 STS)

ROW 1 (RS): [P5, X2R, k4, X2R, p1] across.

ROW 2 (AND ALL WS ROWS THROUGH 20): K the p and p the k sts of the prev row.

ROW 3: [P4, X2R, k4, X2R, p2] across.

ROW 5: [P3, X2R, k4, X2R, p3] across.

ROW 7: [P2, X2R, k4, X2R, p4] across.

ROW 9: [P1, X2R, k4, X2R, p5] across.

ROW 11: [P1, X2L, k4, X2L, p5] across.

ROW 13: [P2, X2L, k4, X2L, p4] across.

ROW 15: [P3, X2L, k4, X2L, p3] across.

ROW 17: [P4, X2L, k4, X2L, p2] across.

ROW 19: [P5, X2L, k4, X2L, p1] across.

Rep Rows 1–20 for patt.

CABLE (6 STS)

ROWS 1, 5 AND 7 (RS): K6.

ROW 2 (AND ALL WS ROWS THROUGH 8): P all sts.

ROW 3: C6B.

Rep Rows 1–8 for patt.

WIDE RIB (MULT OF 7 STS)

ROW 1: [K6, p1] across.

ROW 2: K the p and p the k sts of the prev row.

Rep Rows 1–2 for patt.

Right Front

CO 64 (71, 78) sts.

ROW 1 (RS): [K1, p1] across.

ROW 2: P all sts.

ROW 3: K2, work Row 1 of Zigzag patt over next 28 sts, k2, p1, work Row 1 of Cable patt over next 6 sts, [p1, k6] 3 (4, 5) times, p1, k3.

ROW 4 (AND ALL WS ROWS): K the p and p the k sts of the prev row.

Keep in patt as est in Row 3 of Right Front until Row 3 of Cable patt has been worked 6 times (i.e., the cable has been cabled 6 times). THEN end after Row 2 of Cable patt and work next row as foll:

NEXT ROW (RS): K2, work Zigzag patt over 28 sts, k2, [p1, work Row 3 of Cable patt] 4 (5, 6) times, p1, k3. Stay in this est patt until Cable Row 3 has been worked 6 times in ea ribbing.

NEXT ROW (RS): K2, work Zigzag patt over next 28 sts, k2, p1, work Cable patt over next 6 sts, [p1, k6] 3 (4, 5) times, p1, k3. Stay in this est patt for rest of Front. Work even until piece meas 15" (38cm) from beg.

Armhole Shaping

BO 6 (9, 12) sts at beg of next WS row—58 (62, 66) sts.

BO 3 sts at beg of next WS row—55 (59, 63) sts.

BO 1 st at Armhole Edge every row 5 times—50 (54, 58) sts.

Neck Shaping

When piece meas 16" (41cm) from beg, BO 12 sts at beg of next RS row—38 (42, 46) sts.

BO 3 sts at beg of next row twice—32 (36, 40) sts.

BO 1 st at Neck Edge every row 12 times—20 (24, 28) sts.

Work even until Armhole meas 7½ (7¾, 8)" (19 [20, 20]cm). BO.

Left Front

Work same as Right Front, reversing all shaping, and beg Zigzag patt with Row 11, working Rows 11–19, foll by Rows 1–9, and stay in this patt to top of Front. Work Armhole Shaping at beg of rows on RS, and Neck Shaping at beg of WS rows.

Back

CO 126 (140, 154) sts.

ROW 1 (RS): [K1, p1] across.

ROW 2: P all sts.

ROW 3: K3, *p1, k6; rep from * to last 4 sts, p1, k3.

ROW 4 (AND ALL WS ROWS): K the p and p the k sts of the prev row.

ROW 5: K3, [p1, k6] 3 (4, 5) times, p1, work Row 3 of Cable patt across next 6 sts, [p1, k6] 9 times, p1, work Row 3 of Cable patt across next 6 sts, [p1, k6] 3 (4, 5) times, p1, k3. This establishes the side-back cables; work the Cable at ea side of Back for rest of piece, and keep sts in between in rib.

Keep in patt as est until Row 3 of Cable patt has been worked 6 times (i.e., the cable has been cabled 6 times). THEN after Row 2 of Cable patt work next row as foll:

NEXT ROW (RS): K3, [p1, work Row 3 of Cable patt] 4 (5, 6) times, [p1, k6] 9 times, [p1, work Row 3 of Cable patt] 4 (5, 6) times, p1, k3. Stay in this est patt until Cable Row 3 has been worked 6 times in ea ribbing.

NEXT ROW (RS): K3, [p1, k6] 3 (4, 5) times, p1, work Cable patt over next 6 sts, [p1, k6] 9 times, work Cable patt over next 6 sts, [p1, k6] 3 (4, 5) times p1, k3. Stay in this est patt for rest of Back. Work even until piece meas 15" (38cm) from beg.

Armhole Shaping

BO 6 (9, 12) sts at beg of next 2 rows—114 (122, 130) sts.

BO 3 sts at beg of next 2 rows—108 (116, 124) sts.

BO 1 st at ea Armhole Edge every row 5 times—98 (106, 114) sts. Work even until Armhole meas 5½ (5¾, 6)" (14 [15, 15]cm).

Back Neck

Work across 35 (39, 43) sts then BO center 28 sts. Work to end.

BO 1 st at ea Neck Edge every row 15 times—20 (24, 28) sts.

Work even until Armhole meas 7½ (7¾, 8)" (19 [20, 20]cm). BO.

Finishing

Weave in ends. Block pieces. Sew shoulder seams.

Neck Trim

Using size 0 crochet hook, join yarn at bottom of Right Front Neck Opening and work sc around Right Front, Back and Left Front Neck Edge. Ch 1, turn, [(sc in sc) 3 times, ch 3] across, ending with (sc in sc) 3 times. Fasten off.

Sew side seams. Work crochet around ea Armhole Edge same as for Neck except work continuously around instead of turning.

Button Band

Using size 1 needle and with RS facing, pick up and k 104 sts on Left Front Opening Edge, including side of crochet trim at the top. Work in garter st for 1" (3cm), then BO. Sew on buttons, placing first and last buttons ½" (1cm) in from the edges and 4 rem buttons equally spaced between.

Buttonhole Band

Pick up and k 104 sts along Right Front Opening Edge and work in garter st for ⅜" (1cm), then BO 3 sts opposite ea button for buttonholes. On foll row CO 3 sts over ea gap. BO all sts when band meas 1" (3cm).

To prevent Neckline from gaping:

Cut elastic in half. Gather Neckline while lightly stretching elastic, pin, then hand sew elastic to inside edge of lower Front Neckline on Right and Left Fronts.

Weave in remaining ends.

CRAB APPLE BLOSSOM

The natural drape and soft luster of linen make an elegant cardigan that can be worn in any season. The color of spring blossoms and worsted weight linen combine in an easy-to-knit lace and cable pattern. The body of the sweater is knitted in one piece.

SKILL LEVEL
Intermediate

Note: The easy lace pattern is ideal for the novice lace knitter.

METHOD
Knit

SIZES
To fit actual bust size: 34 (36, 48)" (86 [91, 122]cm)

FINISHED MEASUREMENTS
Bust: Approx 37 (40, 52)" (94 [102, 132]cm)

YARN
7 (8,10) (3½ oz./100g, 190 yd./174m) skeins worsted weight yarn

NEEDLES
47" (120cm) size US 4 (3.5mm) circular needle

Size US 6 (4mm) straight needles

If necessary, change needle size to obtain correct gauge.

NOTIONS
Cable needle

Yarn needle

6 shank buttons, ⅝" (2cm) diameter

GAUGE
18 sts and 30 rows = 4" (10cm) in St st on size US 6 (4mm) needles

Patt rep consisting of one Lace Panel and one Cable Panel = 3¾ (4, 3¾)" (10 [10, 10]cm)

The project shown at right was made using Louet Euroflax, (100% linen, 3½ oz./100g, 190 yd./174m) in Crabapple.

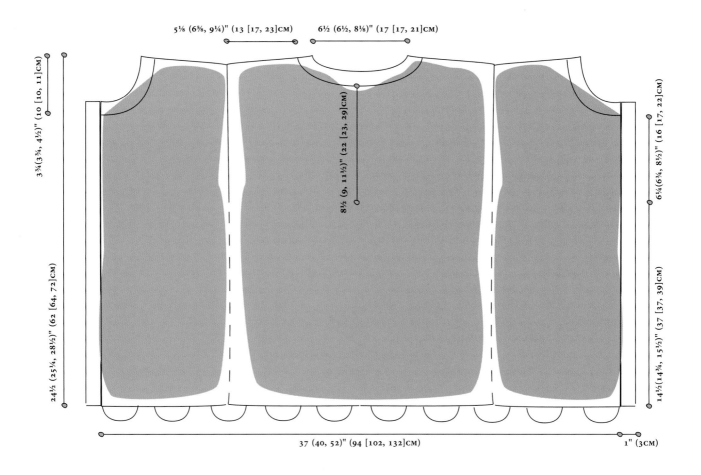

5⅛ (6⅝, 9¼)" (13 [17, 23]cm)   6½ (6½, 8⅛)" (17 [17, 21]cm)

3¾(3¾, 4½)" (10 [10, 11]cm)

8½ (9, 11½)" (22 [23, 29]cm)

6¼(6¾, 8½)" (16 [17, 22]cm)

24½ (25¼, 28½)" (62 [64, 72]cm)

14½(14¾, 15½)" (37 [37, 39]cm)

37 (40, 52)" (94 [102, 132]cm)   1" (3cm)

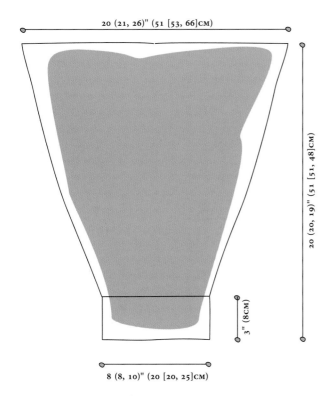

20 (21, 26)" (51 [53, 66]cm)

20 (20, 19)" (51 [51, 48]cm)

3" (8cm)

8 (8, 10)" (20 [20, 25]cm)

ABBREVIATIONS

C4B

Slip 2 sts to cn and hold to back, k2, k2 from cn.

C6B

Slip 3 sts to cn and hold to back, k3, k3 from cn.

PATTERN STITCHES

LACE PANEL (WORKED OVER 12 [14, 12] STS)

ROW 1 (RS): Yo, k4 (5, 4), k2tog, SKP, k4 (5, 4), yo.

ROW 2: P all sts.

Rep Rows 1–2 for patt.

CABLE PANEL (WORKED OVER 8 [10, 8] STS)

ROW 1 (RS): K1, p1, k4 (6, 4), p1, k1.

ROW 2 (AND ALL WS ROWS THROUGH 4): P all sts.

ROW 3 (CABLE ROW): K1, p1, C4B (C6B, C4B), p1, k1.

Rep Rows 1–4, and then work as est for patt, working cable row on every 4th row for Sizes 34 and 38. For Size 36, work Rows 1–2 twice so that cable row is worked every 6th row.

Front and Back

With size 4 needles, CO 194 (232, 274) sts.

ROW 1 (WS): [K1, p1] across.

ROW 2 (RS): K1, *work Lace Panel over 12 (14, 12) sts, work Cable Panel over 8 (10, 8) sts; rep from * across, ending with Lace Panel, k1.

Stay in patt as est, beg and ending ea RS row with k1, and cabling on every 4th row (6th row, 4th row). Work even until piece meas 14½ (14¾, 15½)" (37 [37, 39]cm) (meas from lower edge of a cable panel), ending with a WS row.

Divide for Armholes

NEXT ROW (RS): Staying in patt, work to the center of the 3rd (3rd, 4th) Lace Panel (stop after the k2tog and just before the SKP—47 [56, 67] sts), join a second ball of yarn, work 100 (120, 140) sts across the Back to center of 3rd (3rd, 4th) Lace Panel from the opposite Front, join a third ball of yarn and work to end. Cont to work the two Fronts and the Back of the sweater at the same time with separate balls of yarn until Armholes meas 6¼ (6¾, 8½)" (16 [17, 22]cm).

Front Neck

Cont to work Back even, BO 6 (7, 11) sts at beg of next 2 rows of Fronts. Cont to BO at ea Front edge as foll: 6 sts once, then 3 sts once, then 2 sts once, then 1 st three times.

Back Neck

When Armholes meas 8½ (9, 11½)" (22 [23, 29]cm), BO center 16 (18, 26) sts of Back, join a 4th ball of yarn and cont on all sections.

Working both sides of Back Neck at the same time,

BO 9 sts at Neck edge at beg of next 2 rows.

BO 3 sts at Neck edge at beg of next 2 rows.

BO 1 st at Neck edge at beg of next 2 rows.

Work even until pieces meas 24½ (25¼, 28½)" (62 [64, 72]cm) (meas from lower edge of a Cable Panel). BO.

Sleeves

With size 4 needles, CO 38 (38, 48) sts. Work in garter st for 3" (8cm).

NEXT ROW (RS): Change to size 6 needles and St st and inc 12 (12, 16) sts evenly across row—50 (50, 64) sts. Inc ea side of row every 4th row 8 (12, 22) times—66 (74, 108) sts. Inc every 6th row 12 (10, 4) times—90 (94, 116) sts. Work even until Sleeve meas 20 (20, 19)" (51 [51, 48]cm). BO.

Finishing

Weave in ends. Block pieces. Sew Sleeve seams. Sew Shoulders, then sew the Sleeves into the Armhole openings. With size 4 needles and RS facing, pick up and k 76 (78, 88) sts evenly around Neck. Work in garter st for 1" (3cm). BO.

Button Band

On Left Front with RS facing, pick up and k 99 (103, 115) sts evenly along edge including edge of Neckband, and work in garter st for 1" (3cm). BO. Sew on buttons, placing top and bottom buttons ¾" (2cm) in from upper and lower edges and evenly spacing rem buttons between. (Separate out 1 strand of the linen yarn to use as a sewing thread).

Buttonhole Band

Pick up and k 99 (103, 115) sts along Right Front edge. Work in garter st for ½" (1cm), then BO 2 sts opposite ea button. On foll row, CO 2 sts over gaps. Work even until band meas 1" (3cm). BO.

Weave in remaining ends.

ALMOND SHELL

This Empire-waist sweater in organic cotton is rich in charm and details and feels so soft! It features a scoop neck finished in softly rounded Reverse Stockinette Stitch, a sideways knitted peplum and flared sleeve cuffs. Tied cordings accent the shaping. The floral embroidery is optional.

SKILL LEVEL
Intermediate

METHOD
Knit

SIZES
To fit actual bust size: 35 (38, 40)" (89 [97, 102]cm)

FINISHED MEASUREMENTS
Bust: Approx same as Sizes

YARN
8 (8, 9) (2¼ oz./65g, 150 yd./137m) skeins sport weight yarn

NEEDLES
Size US 4 (3.5mm) straight needles

Size US 5 (3.75mm) straight needles

40" (100cm) size US 5 circular needle

If necessary, change needle size to obtain correct gauge.

HOOK
Size US E/4 (3.5mm) crochet hook

NOTIONS
Stitch holder

Yarn needle

GAUGE
22 sts and 28 rows = 4" (10cm) in St st on size US 5 (3.75mm) needles

The project shown at right was made using Blue Sky Skinny Organic (100% color grown cotton, 2¼ oz./65g, 150 yd./137m) in color 31 Clay.

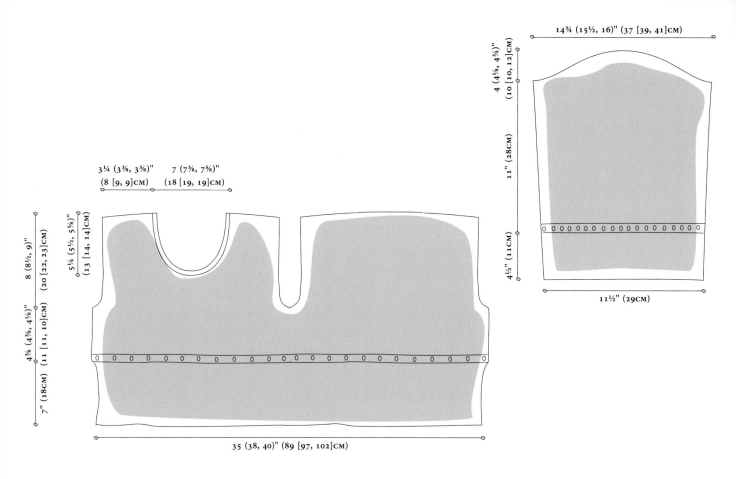

PATTERN STITCH

REVERSE STOCKINETTE STITCH (MULT OF 1 ST)

ROW 1 (RS): P all sts.

ROW 2: K all sts.

Rep Rows 1–2 for patt.

Peplum

Using size 4 needles, CO 36 sts.

ROW 1 (RS): K across, turning and working short rows over final 12 sts. (On the second rep, work short rows over final 18 sts, and then alternate between 12 and 18 sts for the length of the piece.)

ROWS 2, 4, 7 AND 11: P all sts.

ROWS 3, 5, 6, 8, 10 AND 12: K all sts.

ROW 9: K2, *yo, k2tog; rep from * across.

Rep Rows 1–12 a total of 24 (26, 28) times; piece meas approx 37 (40, 43)" (94 [102, 109]cm). BO all sts.

Front and Back

Using size 5 circular needle and with RS facing, pick up and k along the upper edge of the Peplum 8 sts for ea rep of the Peplum pattern—192 (208, 224) sts. Tie on a short length of contrasting yarn after the 96th (104th, 112th) st to mark the second side seam placement.

Work the foll 7 rows for Eyelet Casing:

Eyelet Casing

ROW 1 (WS): K all sts.

ROWS 2 AND 6: P all sts.

ROWS 3, 5 AND 7: K all sts.

ROW 4: P, and to create Eyelet holes for the tie-cord, work [yo, p2tog], centering ea yo directly above ea vertical yo row of the Peplum.

ROW 8: Change to St st and work even for 4½ (4½, 4)" (11 [11, 10]cm), meas from the upper edge of the Eyelet Casing (the St st portion only).

Armhole Shaping

At beg of next row, BO 3 (4, 6) sts, then work up to the placement of the tied-on marker (foll the line of sts on up). Join a second ball of yarn and work the same number of BO sts foll the marker, work to end of row.

At beg of next row work same number of BO sts, and again foll the marker placement, work to end of row.

Then make the foll BO sts at beg of ea Armhole edge:

SIZE 35: BO 1 st at ea Armhole edge 6 times—78 sts rem on ea side.

SIZE 38: BO 2 sts at ea Armhole edge twice, then 1 st 4 times—80 sts rem on ea side.

SIZE 40: BO 2 sts at ea Armhole edge, then 1 st 6 times—84 sts rem on ea side.

Work even until 7⅛ (7½, 7⅝)" (18 [19, 19]cm) above Eyelet Casing.

Neck Shaping

Decide which half of the knitted piece will be the Front. BO 10 (14, 14) sts at the center of the Front, joining a third ball of yarn. Cont shaping the Neck opening as foll:

SIZE 35: BO 4 sts at ea edge once, then 3 sts once, then 1 st 7 times—38 sts bound off.

SIZES 38 & 40: BO 3 sts at ea edge once, then 2 sts twice, then 1 st 6 times—40 (40) sts bound off.

Shoulder Shaping

When Armhole meas 7¼ (7⅝, 8)" (18 [19, 20]cm), BO 5 (5, 7) sts at ea side edge, then 5 sts at ea Shoulder 3 times—20 (20, 22) sts bound off on ea Shoulder.

Place the rem 39 (40, 42) Back Neck sts on a holder.

Sleeves

Using size 4 needles, CO 24 sts and foll the pattern for Peplum, working short rows over 12 sts throughout. Complete 8 reps of the patt, then BO.

Using size 5 straight needles, along the upper edge with RS facing, pick up and k 8 sts for ea rep of st patt—64 sts. Work Rows 1–3 of Eyelet Casing.

ROW 4 OF EYELET CASING FOR SLEEVE: *P2, yo, p2tog; rep from * to end.

Work Rows 5–7 of Eyelet Casing.

Change to St st.

SIZE 40 ONLY: Inc 4 sts evenly in first row of St st.

ALL SIZES: Inc 1 st ea side every 6th row 8 (10, 10) times—80 (84, 88) sts. Work even until Sleeve meas 11" (28cm) from upper edge of Eyelet Casing.

Sleeve Cap

BO 4 sts at beg of next 2 rows 1 (1, 2) times—72 (76, 72) sts.

BO 3 sts at beg of next 2 rows 1 (2, 1) times—66 (64, 66) sts.

BO 2 sts at beg of next 2 rows 4 (5, 2) times—50 (44, 58) sts.

BO 1 st at beg of next 2 rows 4 (4, 7) times—42 (36, 44) sts.

BO 2 sts at beg of next 2 rows 2 (1, 3) times—34 (32, 32) sts.

BO 3 sts at beg of next 2 rows 1 (1, 2) times—28 (26, 20) sts.

SIZES 35 & 38: BO 4 sts at beg of next 2 rows. BO rem 20 (18) sts.

SIZE 40: BO rem 20 sts.

Finishing

Weave in ends. Block pieces. Sew one Shoulder.

Neck Trim

Using size 4 needles, on RS, pick up and k 81 (86, 86) sts evenly spaced around Front Neck edge, plus the 39 (40, 42) sts on the holder for the Back Neck—120 (126, 128) sts. Work in Reverse Stockinette Stitch for 1" (3cm). BO.

Sew rem Shoulder and ends of Neck trim. Loosely stitch the long edge of Neck trim to the picked up edge. Set in Sleeves. Sew side and Sleeve seams.

Cordings

Using size E/4 crochet hook, make a chain 28" (71cm) long, turn. Sl st in ea ch. Fasten off. Rep for second cord. Thread the cordings through the Sleeve Eyelets, beg and ending opposite the Sleeve seam. Fit the cording so your hand can slide through the Sleeve, then tie a bow. Make a third cording 60" (152cm) long and thread through the Eyelets of the sweater body and tie a bow in front.

Embroidery (optional)

Using the same yarn as for the sweater, randomly embroider Lazy Daisy stitch flowers, 6 petals for ea and making ea flower approx ¾"–1" (2–3cm) across. Place them around the Neck opening and on the Back, and several above the tie on ea Sleeve.

Weave in remaining ends.

MIDNIGHT FLOWERS

This classy linen mesh scarf sports Irish Crochet blooms. This one has three flowers and leaves, but you can make more (or even just one) if you like. Light weight linen works beautifully for fine crochet.

SKILL LEVEL
Experienced

METHOD
Crochet

SIZE
One size

FINISHED MEASUREMENTS
Approx 4" × 38" (10cm × 97cm)

YARN
1 (3½ oz./100g, 580 yd./530m) cone lace weight yarn

Size 8 pearl cotton in assorted colors for flowers and leaves

HOOKS
Size 3 (2.1mm) steel crochet hook

Size 7 (1.65mm) steel crochet hook

NOTIONS
Yarn needle

Sewing needle

Thread to match yarn

GAUGE
Not important for this project

The project shown at right was made using Louet Euroflax 14/2, (100% linen, 3½ oz./100g, 580 yd./530m) in color 22 Black.

Scarf

ROW 1: Using size 3 hook and lace weight yarn, ch 4. Dc into first ch.

ROW 2: Ch 5, turn. Sc in the ch-4 lp of prev row, ch 2, dc in second-to-last ch of lp.

ROW 3: Ch 5, turn. Sc in first lp, ch 3, sc in next lp, ch 2, dc in second-to-last ch of final lp.

ROW 4: Ch 5, turn. Sc in first lp, [ch 3, sc in lp] across to and including final lp, ch 2, dc in second-to-last ch of lp.

Rep Row 4 until there are 10 lps across.

NEXT ROW: Ch 4, turn, sc in lp, [ch 3, sc in lp] across. Rep last row until Scarf meas 26" (66cm).

MAKE OPENING: Ch 4, turn. [Sc in lp, ch 3] 5 times, sc in next lp, ch 12, skip 3 lps, sc in next lp. Work to end of row as before. Work next row as before up to the ch-12 lp. Ch 3 and sc into second ch, [ch 3, skip 2 ch, sc] 3 times, ch 3 and sc into next ch-3 lp of row and work to end.

Cont in est patt until Scarf meas 31" (79cm).

NEXT ROW: Ch 1, turn. Sl st into first lp, ch 1, sc, [ch 3, sc] across.

Rep last row until one ch-3 lp rem. Fasten off.

Finishing

Edging
In ea space around outer edge of Scarf work (2 sc, ch 3, 2 sc).

Irish Rose
Use 3 colors for ea Rose—I suggest yellow for the center and 2 petal colors as desired.

Using size 7 hook and yellow pearl cotton, ch 4 and join to form a ring.

RND 1: Ch 1 and work 8 sc in ring, join to top of first sc with a sl st.

RND 2: Ch 1 and work 16 sc into the ring over the prev rnd of 8 sc. Join with sl st to the first sc of Rnd 2.

RND 3: Ch 1, sc in same space, [ch 4, skip 1, sc in next sc] 8 times, sl st into beg sc. Fasten off.

RND 4: Join a 2nd color in one of the ch-4 lps and work (sc, hdc, 3 dc, hdc, sc) into the lp. Rep for ea of the ch-4 lps.

RND 5: [Sc in back of the prev rnd between petals, ch 5] 8 times, then sl st into beg sc.

RND 6: Into ea ch-5 lp work (sc, hdc, 4 dc, hdc, sc). Fasten off.

RND 7: With a 3rd color, sc in back of the prev rnd between petals. [Ch 6, sc between petals] 8 times, then sl st into beg sc.

RND 8: Into ea ch-6 lp work (sc, hdc, dc, 4 tr, dc, hdc, sc). Fasten off.

Leaf
Using size 7 hook and the pearl cotton you've chosen for the leaves, ch 12.

Sc in 2nd ch from hk forming the Leaf tip, then sc in next 9 ch. In end ch work (sc, ch 3, sc), then sc in next 8 ch along opposite side of starting ch. Ch 3, turn.

Working into both lps of ea sc, sc in next 9 sts. In the ch 3 at the end work (sc, ch 3, sc). Sc in next 8 sts on opposite side of Leaf. Ch 3, turn.

From here on work in back lp of ea sc. Sc in next 9 sts, at end work (sc, ch 3, sc), sc in next 8 sts. Ch 3, turn. Rep this row until there are 5 Leaf tips on ea side of Leaf. Fasten off.

Stem
Using size 7 hook and the pearl cotton you've chosen for the flower stems, make a ch 9" (23cm) long. Turn and sc along ch. Work 3 sc into end ch, then sc along opposite side of the starting ch.

Lightly press Roses, Leaves and Stem. Arrange the Stem on the Scarf, then place the Leaves and Roses along the Stem. Pin in place. Working on the back of the Scarf, and with needle and matching thread, sew the pieces in place. Weave in ends.

SEAWEED IN FRILLS

Encase your neck in this silky boa—wrap twice and tuck in the ends, or just tie it into a loose knot. The boa is worked in the round, then the center of the round is brought together and sewn.

SKILL LEVEL Beginner	**FINISHED MEASUREMENTS** Approx 43" (109cm) long	**NEEDLES** 47" (120cm) size US 4 (3.5mm) circular needle
METHOD Knit		
SIZE One size	**YARN** 1 (3½ oz./100g, 274 yd./250m) skein DK weight yarn	**NOTIONS** Stitch marker Yarn needle
		GAUGE Not important for this project

The project shown at right was made using Hand Maiden Double Sea Silk (70% silk/30% Seacell, 3½ oz./100g, 274 yd./250m) in Safari.

Boa

CO 256 sts. Place marker and join in a rnd, being careful not to twist the sts.

Note: The stitch counts provided below are given to show the amount of increasing that is done. Beyond the cast-on row, don't worry about the stitch count, though.

RNDS 1–2: K all sts.

RND 3: [K1, yo] around—512 sts.

RNDS 4–5: K all sts.

RNDS 6–8: Rep Rnds 3–5—1,024 sts.

RND 9: Inc in ea st around—2,048 sts.

BO.

Finishing

Bring center tog (halves of cast-on row touching) and sew a seam along cast-on row for length of boa. Weave in ends. Allow to curl into ruffles.

BIRCH BARK

This man's vest is inspired by the textures and multihued shades of tree bark. The linen and cotton vest will go great with khakis, with or without a tie. The fronts are worked from the bottom up, and the back is knitted from side to side. The softness of cotton and the luster of linen combine to make a beautiful fabric.

SKILL LEVEL
Experienced

METHOD
Knit

SIZES
To fit actual chest size: 42–44 (46–48, 50–52)" (107–112 [117–122, 127–132]cm)

FINISHED MEASUREMENTS
Chest: Approx 47 (54, 58)" (119 [137, 147]cm)

YARN
9 (12, 15) (1¾ oz./50g, 93 yd./85m) skeins worsted weight yarn, 5 (6, 7) skeins MC, 2 (3, 4) skeins ea CC1 and CC2

NEEDLES
Size US 4 (3.5mm) straight needles

Size US 1 (2.25mm) straight needles

32" (80cm) or 40" (100cm) size US 1 (2.25mm) circular needle

If necessary, change needle size to obtain correct gauge.

NOTIONS
Yarn needle

6 wooden buttons, ⅝" (2cm) diameter

GAUGE
Front: 20 sts and 36 rows = 4" (10cm) in patt on size US 4 (3.5mm) needles

Back: 20 sts and 32 rows = 4" (10cm) in patt on size US 4 (3.5mm) needles

The project shown at right was made using Garnstudio Bomull/Lin (53% cotton/47% linen, 1¾ oz./50g, 93 yd./85m) in colors 03 (MC), 02 (CC1) and 05 (CC2).

ESTABLISHING GAUGE FOR SWEATER BACK

The back of the vest is knitted from side seam to side seam, and knitted fabric stretches the most on the lengthwise grain. Cotton and linen have no "bounce-back" capacity, so the gauge swatch needs special treatment to get it to the same place it will end up in blocking and wearing. Knit a good-sized swatch—6–8" (15–20cm) square. Wash and dry the swatch, then hold it up by one side edge and gently tug on it until it is relaxed to where it will naturally be when worn. Then take the gauge.

7½ (7¾, 8)" (19 [20, 20]CM)

23½ (27, 29)" (60 [69, 74]CM)

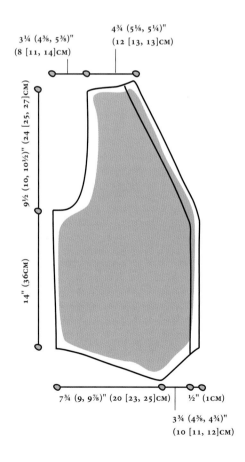

3¼ (4⅜, 5⅜)"
(8 [11, 14]CM)

4¾ (5⅛, 5¼)"
(12 [13, 13]CM)

9½ (10, 10½)" (24 [25, 27]CM)

14" (36CM)

7¾ (9, 9⅞)" (20 [23, 25]CM)

½" (1CM)

3¾ (4⅜, 4¾)"
(10 [11, 12]CM)

PATTERN STITCHES

STITCH AND COLOR PATTERN FOR FRONT SECTIONS

Note: When keeping in patt, note the placement of the p sts in Row 7. If the p sts are placed differently in relation to Rows 1–6, the knitted texture will be different from intended.

Work Rows 1–6 in MC. Work Rows 7–8 in CC1 alternating with CC2 as shown in graphs on pages 94–95.

ROW 1 (RS): [K1, bring yarn to front, sl1 pwise and bring yarn to back] across.

ROWS 2, 4, 6 AND 8: P all sts.

ROW 3: [Bring yarn to front, sl1 pwise and bring yarn to back, k1] across.

ROW 5: Rep Row 1.

ROW 7: [P1, k1] across.

Rep Rows 1–8 for patt.

COLOR PATTERN FOR BACK

Work [2 rows in MC, 2 in CC1, 2 in MC, 2 in CC2] and rep throughout. When changing colors, if stranding is less than 1" (3cm), run the yarns along the edges of the knitting. If longer, cut and work the ends in afterwards.

REVERSE STOCKINETTE STITCH (MULT OF 1 ST)

ROW 1 (RS): P all sts.

ROW 2: K all sts.

Rep Rows 1–2 for patt.

1×1 RIB (MULT OF 2 STS)

ROW 1: *K1, p1; rep from * across.

Rep Row 1 for patt.

Right Front and Left Front

Using size 4 needles, CO 4 (5, 5) sts. The graphs on pages 94–95 give the Stitch and Color Pattern beg at the bottom points of the vest Fronts. Foll the Stitch and Color Pattern, and inc as directed. Keep in patt for the rest of the Front sections as given above the vest points in the graph.

Neck Shaping

Work even until side seam meas 13" (33cm), then beg BO for Neck. BO 1 st at Neck edge every ½" (1cm) 21 (21, 22) times, then work even to top of Shoulder. AT THE SAME TIME, beg Armhole Shaping.

Armhole Shaping

When side seam meas 14" (36cm), beg BO at Armhole edge. At the beg of ea row BO 6 (6, 9) sts once, then 0 (4, 4) sts once, then 2 sts 1 (2, 2) times, then 1 st 7 (7, 8) times—15 (21, 25) sts bound off. Work even to Shoulder Shaping—20 (23, 23) sts rem.

Shoulder Shaping

When Armhole meas 9½ (10, 10½)" (24 [25, 27]cm), beg shoulder BO at Armhole edge:

SIZE 40: BO 4 sts 5 times.

SIZE 46: BO 4 sts 3 times, then 3 sts twice, then 5 sts.

SIZE 50: BO 4 sts twice, then 3 sts 5 times at beg of row at left edge.

Back

The back is worked in Reverse Stockinette Stitch beg at a side seam.

Using size 4 needles, CO 67 sts in MC, and p the first row (RS). Keep in Color Pattern for Back throughout.

Armhole Shaping

When piece meas 1¼ (2, 2)" (3 [5, 5]cm) beg inc for Armhole.

Inc 1 st at beg of next RS row 2 (4, 5) times—69 (71, 72) sts.

Inc 2 sts at beg of next RS row 3 (2, 3) times—75 (75, 81) sts.

Inc 3 sts at beg of next RS row 1 (2, 2) times—78 (82, 87) sts.

Inc 5 sts at beg of next RS row—83 (87, 92) sts.

Piece should meas approx 3¼ (4½, 5)" (8 [11, 13]cm) from beg.

At beg of next RS row inc 31 (31, 30) sts evenly across—114 (118, 120 sts).

Shoulder Shaping

Inc 1 st every 4 rows 6 (7, 8) times—120 (125, 128) sts. Work even until piece meas 7¼ (9½, 9¾)" (18 [24, 28]cm) from beg. Tie on a scrap of yarn to mark the start of the Neck area.

Work even for 9 (10, 9¾)" (23 [25, 25]cm) from marker and tie on a second scrap to mark the end of the Neck area. (Keep markers in place until Finishing.)

Mirror the shaping for Shoulder and Armhole, working dec in place of inc at beg of WS rows. BO 67 sts.

Finishing

Weave in ends. Sew Shoulder seams.

Armhole Edgings

Using size 1 circular needle and with MC and RS facing, pick up and k 4½ sts per 1" (3cm) (9 sts over 2" [5cm]). BO kwise.

Sew side seams.

Vest Bottom Edging

Using size 1 circular needle and with MC and RS facing, pick up and k 4½ sts per 1" (3cm) (9 sts over 2" [5cm]), starting at one Front opening edge and going across Front bottom edge, picking up an extra st at vest points, across Back bottom edge, and other Front bottom edge ending at opposite Front opening edge.

BO kwise (on WS) along Front bottom edges, and BO in 1×1 Rib along Back section, and back again to BO kwise along rem Front sts.

Neck Band

Using size 1 circular needle, MC and RS facing and starting at one lower edge of Front opening, pick up and k 4½ sts per 1" (3cm) (9 sts over 2" [5cm]), going up Front opening edge—picking up an extra st at the points where dec beg for Neck Shaping, around back of Neck, and down the opposite side ending at the Bottom edge.

Work 1 row in 1×1 Rib, change to CC1 and work 2 rows. Change to MC for the next row and on the Left Front Band, work 6 buttonholes by binding off 3 sts at the foll locations: the first ½" (1cm) below the beg of Neck Shaping, the last ¾" (2cm) above the bottom of the Band, with the rem 4 evenly spaced between the first and last. Work the next row in MC, casting on 3 sts over ea buttonhole. Change to CC2 and work 2 rows, change to MC and work 1 row, then BO in Rib. Sew buttons to Right Front Band, opposite the buttonholes on the Left Front Band.

Back Ties (make 2)

Using size 4 needles and MC, CO 50 sts. Work in 1×1 Rib for 4 rows, then BO all sts. Sew to ea side of Back at waistline.

Weave in remaining ends.

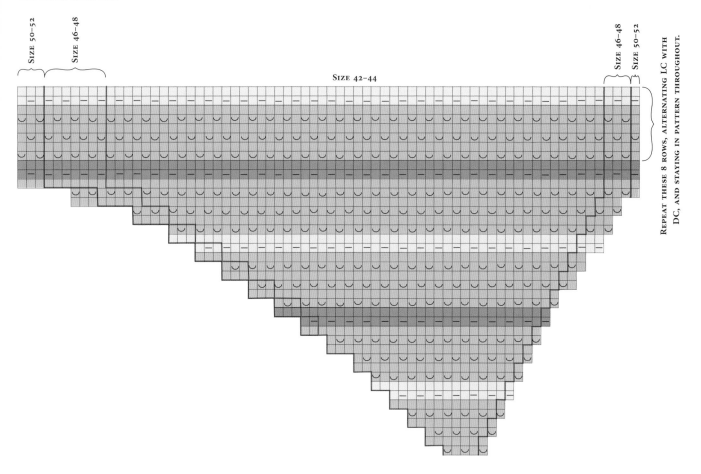

Size 50–52 Size 46–48 Size 42–44 Size 46–48 Size 50–52

REPEAT THESE 8 ROWS, ALTERNATING LC WITH DC, AND STAYING IN PATTERN THROUGHOUT.

VEST CHART KEY

⌣ YARN FORWARD, SLIP 1 PURLWISE, YARN BACK

▢ KNIT ON RS, PURL ON WS

— PURL ON RS

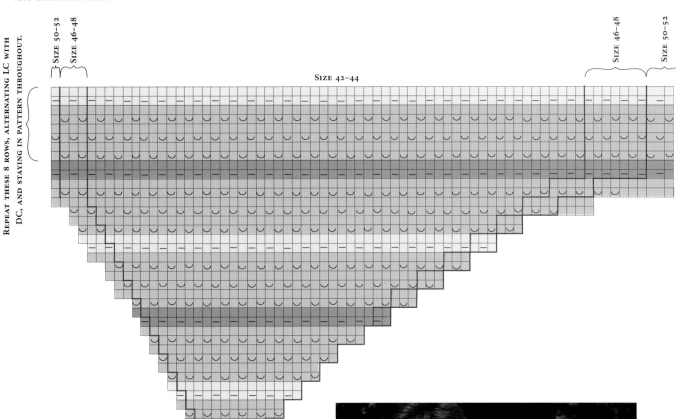

YARROW

This Tweed-stitch tie is made of a cotton yarn that seems engineered to produce a distinctive and suave finish.

SKILL LEVEL
Intermediate

METHOD
Knit and Crochet

SIZE
One size

FINISHED MEASUREMENTS
Approx 53"
(135cm) long

YARN
2 (1¾ oz./50g, 109 yd./100m) skeins
DK weight yarn

NEEDLES
Size US 4 (3.5mm)
straight needles

If necessary, change needle size to obtain correct gauge.

HOOK
Size US D/3
(3.25mm)
crochet hook

NOTIONS
Yarn needle

GAUGE
24 sts and 28 rows
= 4" (10cm) in St
st on size US 4
(3.5mm) needles

*The project shown at right was made using Garnstudio Muskat
(100% cotton, 1¾ oz./50g, 109 yd./100m) in color 08.*

TWEED (MULT OF 2 STS)

ROW 1 (RS): [K1, move yarn to front, sl1 pwise, move yarn to back] across.

ROWS 2 AND 4: P all sts.

ROW 3: [Move yarn to front, sl1 pwise, move yarn to back, k1] across.

Rep Rows 1–4 for patt. Be careful to stay in patt when working Tweed stitch—moving the yarn forward creates a horizontal bar that alternates on every other row.

Tie

Using size 4 needles, CO 3 sts.

ROW 1 (WS): K all sts.

ROW 2 (RS): K1, inc in next st, k1—4 sts.

Note: Incs are worked by knitting into the front, then the back of a st.

ROW 3: K all sts.

ROW 4: K1, [inc in next st] twice, k1—6 sts.

ROW 5: K2, p2, k2 and from here on, on all WS rows, k2 at ea edge, and p the sts between.

ROW 6: K1, [inc in next st] 4 times, k1—10 sts.

ROW 8: K1, [inc in next st] twice, work next 4 sts in Tweed patt, [inc in next st] twice, k1—14 sts.

ROW 10: K1, [inc in next st] twice, work in Tweed patt to last 3 sts, [inc in next st] twice, k1.

Rep Row 10 until there are 30 sts (widest point of Tie).

NEXT RS ROW: K1, k2tog, work in Tweed patt to last 3 sts, k2tog, k1—28 sts.

NEXT RS ROW: K2, work in Tweed patt to last 2 sts, k2. Rep this row on RS until piece meas 2" (5cm) above widest point of Tie.

From here on dec 1 st every 1½" (4cm), alternating the foll dec rows to be on every other side of RS rows (it may be helpful to mark the last-made dec with a safety pin):

DEC ROW FOR RIGHT EDGE: K1, k2tog, work in Tweed patt to last 2 sts, k2.

DEC ROW FOR LEFT EDGE: K2, work in Tweed patt to last 3 sts, k2tog, k1.

Work in this manner until 8 sts rem. Work even on these 8 sts until Tie meas 39" (99cm) from beg, ending with a WS row.

NEXT ROW (RS): K1, inc in next st, work in Tweed patt to last 2 sts, inc in next st, k1. Rep this inc row every 2" (5cm) until Tie meas 51" (130cm) and there are 14 sts, ending with a WS row.

NEXT ROW (RS): K1, k2tog, work in Tweed patt to last 3 sts, k2tog, k1.

NEXT ROW (WS): K2, p to last 2 sts, k2.

Rep prev two rows until 6 sts rem.

NEXT ROW (RS): K1, [k2tog] twice, k1.

NEXT ROW (WS): [P2tog] twice.

NEXT ROW: K2tog and fasten off.

Finishing

Using size D/3 crochet hook and beg at approx the back neck area, join yarn and sl st around, working into the vertical threads and skipping the bumps at the ends of rows, working an extra 1 or 2 sts at the points. Weave in ends. Block Tie using steam iron on medium heat on WS of tie.

PALM LEAF

Less than one skein of yarn is needed to make this elegant and cozy neck warmer. Banana fiber is both soft and weighty, so a small piece like this is a perfect project for it. Choose a special button to fasten it with, or eliminate the buttonhole and fasten with a pretty brooch.

SKILL LEVEL Beginner	**YARN** 1 (7 oz./200g, 150 yd./137m) skein heavy worsted weight yarn	**NOTIONS** Yarn needle 1 button, 2" (5cm) diameter
METHOD Knit		
SIZE One size	**NEEDLES** Size US 11 (8mm) straight needles	**GAUGE** 10½ sts and 12 rows = 4" (10cm) in St st
FINISHED MEASUREMENTS 9" × 21" (23cm × 53cm)	*If necessary, change needle size to obtain correct gauge.*	

The project shown at right was made using Frabjous Fibers Banana Silk Yarn (100% rayon made from banana tree cellulose, 7 oz./200g, 150 yd./137m) in color 04.

Neck Warmer
CO 24 sts. Work in St st, p first and last st on RS rows. Work even for 18" (46cm), ending with a WS row.

NEXT ROW (RS): K4, BO 2 sts, k to end.

On WS, CO 2 sts over the bound-off sts, then work even until piece measures 21" (53cm). BO.

Finishing
Weave in ends. Sew button opposite buttonhole.

ZINNIA

Knit this fitted halter top for hot summer days. Instructions allow you to "fit as you knit" because every body is different. The corn yarn creates a cool, comfortable, machine-washable garment that is perfect for warm summer days.

SKILL LEVEL
Intermediate

METHOD
Knit and Crochet

SIZES
To fit actual bust size: 34 (38)" (91 [102]cm) as written, with extended sizing instructions in the Notes

FINISHED MEASUREMENTS
Bust: Approx 34 (38)" (86 [97]cm)

YARN
4 (5) (1¼ oz./35g, 100 yd./91m) skeins worsted weight yarn

NEEDLES
Size US 6 (4mm) straight needles

40" (100cm) size US 6 circular needle

If necessary, change needle size to obtain correct gauge.

HOOK
Size US D/3 (3.25mm) crochet hook

NOTIONS
4 buttons, ¾" (2cm) diameter

1½ yd. (1.5m) of ⅜" (1cm) elastic

Large safety pin

Stitch holder

Yarn needle

GAUGE
20 sts and 28 rows = 4" (10cm) slightly stretched in 2×1 Rib pattern on size US 6 (4mm) needles

The project shown at right was made using Kollage Cornucopia (100% corn, 1¼ oz./35g, 100 yd./91m) in Gold.

ABBREVIATIONS

INCK

Inc by working k, then p into front of st.

INCP

Inc by working p, then k into front of st.

On the foll (WS) row, p the k, and k the p parts of the inc.

PATTERN STITCHES

2×1 RIB (MULT OF 3 + 2 STS)

ROW 1 (RS): *K2, p1; rep from * to last 2 sts, k2.

ROW 2: *P2, k1; rep from * to last 2 sts, p2.

Rep Rows 1–2 for patt.

1×1 RIB (MULT OF 2 STS)

ROW 1: *K1, p1; rep from * across.

Rep Row 1 for patt.

First Front Section

Beg at Back Neck, CO 11 sts. Work in 2×1 Rib for 1" (3cm), ending with a WS row. Beg to inc as foll:

INC ROW 1 (RS): K2, incK into next st, k2 and cont in 2×1 Rib across row to 3 sts from end, incP into next st, end k2—13 sts.

NEXT ROW (WS): P3, work in 2×1 Rib to last 3 sts, p3.

Work in patt as est until piece meas 2" (5cm), ending with a WS row.

INC ROW 2 (RS): K3, incK, work in 2×1 Rib to last 4 sts, incP, k3—15 sts.

NEXT ROW (WS): P4, work in 2×1 Rib to last 4 sts, p4.

Work in 2×1 Rib as est until piece meas 3" (8cm), ending with a WS row.

Note: Shaping as given is for average size bodies. The pattern of increases can be "stepped up" for larger bosoms. Measure across bust from side seam to side seam and multiply this number by 5 (the stitch gauge) for the number of sts needed. Make the needed changes after the initial 3" (8cm) of the halter.

INC ROW 3 (RS): K2, p1, k1, incK, work in 2×1 Rib to last 5 sts, incP, k1, p1, k2—17 sts.

NEXT ROW (WS): [P2, k1] across, ending with p2.

Thereafter rep the 3 inc rows every ½" (1cm) until piece meas 11 (12)" (28 [30]cm) and there are 47 (51) sts. Place the sts on a holder.

Second Front Section

Pick up and k 11 sts along the CO sts at Back Neck, then k the second Front to match the first. Try the halter on and make sure the ends are even with your armpits. If the halter is too short, add extra rows.

Back

Note: To custom-fit the Back section, measure your back from side seam to side seam just below armpits. Multiply by 5 (the stitch gauge) for the number of sts needed.

Change to the circular needle, and cont from where the yarn is on the section of Front that is being knitted, CO 76 (85) sts (or the number needed for Back)—170 (187) sts. (If you changed the number of sts make sure your back sts are a multiple of 3 + 1.) Work across the other Front section so the circular needle holds a Front, the Back, and the other Front as a continuous unit.

Work back and forth in 2×1 Rib until piece meas 5" (13cm) from top of Back, ending with a WS row.

Waist Shaping

NEXT ROW (RS): Dec in the second, and then every third rib, ending with k2 as foll: [k2, p1, k2tog, p1, k2, p1, k2, p1] across, ending k2.

NEXT ROW: K the p and p the k sts of prev row. Cont in this manner until piece meas 7 (8)" (18 [20]cm) from top of back. BO.

Finishing

Elastic Casing

Using a circular needle, pick up and k around entire Back opening starting at Back Neck. Work in 1×1 Rib for 2 rows, then BO in patt. Fold the ribbing to the back and lightly stitch in place, leaving an opening to insert elastic. Fasten a large safety pin to the end of the elastic and work it through the casing. When it is evenly around without stretching, stretch very slightly and pin. Try on the halter. Adjust the elastic until it fits comfortably. Trim the elastic ends and overlap them about ½" (1cm). Using sewing thread, stitch ends tog, then finish sewing the casing.

Front Opening

Using crochet hook and working into 2 loops of the knitted sts, sc evenly along the Front opening, starting at one bottom edge and working around to the other. Check that the crochet neither bunches nor stretches the knitted edge. Do not fasten off.

Button Band

Ch 1, turn, and sc up to the level of the final inc of the upper section of the halter. Sc back and forth until 6 rows are worked. Fasten off. Sew buttons ½" (1cm) from ea end and 2 buttons evenly spaced between.

Buttonhole Band

Fasten to bottom of rem Front and work 2 rows of sc.

ROW 3: [Ch 2, skip 2 sts] opposite ea button. On the foll row, sc, working 1 sc into ea ch. Work 2 more rows of sc, then fasten off.

Weave in ends.

SAGE

Pair your crochet skills with knitting to make this casual tee. Or, eliminate the crochet and make the knitted front and back longer for an all-knitted top (purchase extra yarn if you decide to knit the entire top). This piece is knitted in the round up to the armholes.

SKILL LEVEL
Knitting:
Beginner

Crochet:
Intermediate

METHOD
Knit and Crochet

SIZES
To fit actual bust
size: 34 (36, 39,
42, 46)" (86 [91,
99, 107, 117]cm)

FINISHED MEASUREMENTS
Bust: Approx 38½
(40¾, 44, 47¼,
52)" (98 [104, 112,
120, 132]cm)

YARNS
4 (5, 5, 6, 7) (3½
oz./100g, 150
yd./137m) skeins
worsted weight
yarn (A)

1 (16 oz./450g,
2,110 yd./1,911m)
cone fingering
weight yarn (B)

NEEDLES
Size US 7 (4.5mm)
straight needles

32" (81cm)
US 7 (4.5mm)
circular needle

Size US 5
(3.75mm)
straight needles

*If necessary,
change needle
size to obtain
correct gauge.*

HOOK
Size 1 (2.75mm)
steel crochet hook

NOTIONS
Stitch markers

Stitch holder

Yarn needle

GAUGE
16 sts and 24 rows
= 4" (10cm) in
St st with Yarn
A on size US 7
(4.5mm) needles

One rep of
crochet patt =
1⅝" (4cm) across

The project shown at right was made using Blue Sky Dyed Organic Cotton (100% organic cotton, 3½ oz./100g, 150 yd./137m) in color 626 Stone (A) and Valley Yarns 5/2 Pearl Cotton (100% mercerized cotton, 16 oz./450g, 2,110 yd./1,911m) in color 7503 Shell (B).

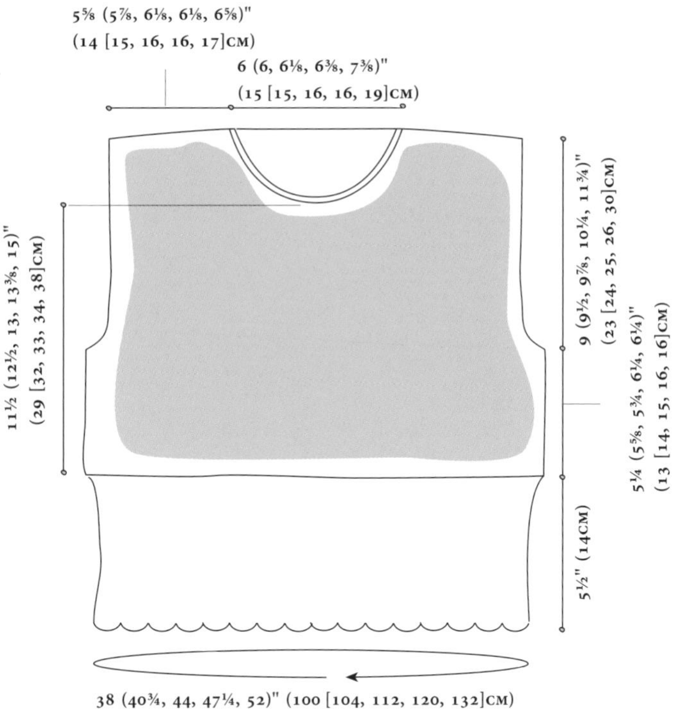
5⅝ (5⅞, 6⅛, 6⅛, 6⅝)"
(14 [15, 16, 16, 17]cm)
6 (6, 6⅛, 6⅜, 7⅜)"
(15 [15, 16, 16, 19]cm)
11½ (12½, 13, 13⅜, 15)"
(29 [32, 33, 34, 38]cm)
9 (9½, 9⅞, 10¼, 11¾)"
(23 [24, 25, 26, 30]cm)
5¼ (5⅝, 5¾, 6¼, 6¼)"
(13 [14, 15, 16, 16]cm)
5½" (14cm)
38 (40¾, 44, 47¼, 52)" (100 [104, 112, 120, 132]cm)

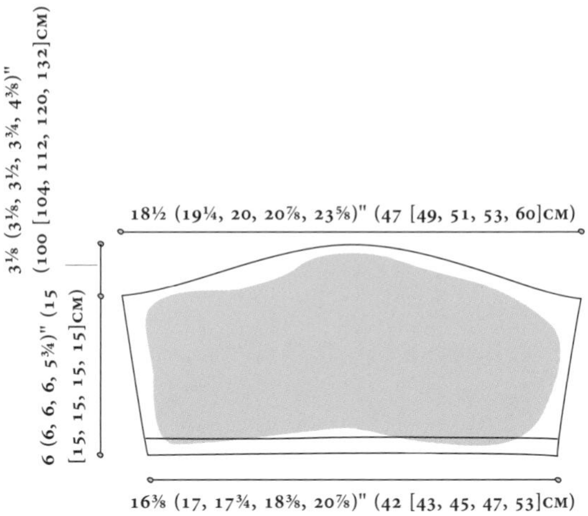
3⅛ (3⅜, 3½, 3¾, 4⅜)"
(100 [104, 112, 120, 132]cm)
18½ (19¼, 20, 20⅞, 23⅝)" (47 [49, 51, 53, 60]cm)
6 (6, 6, 6, 5¾)" (15
[15, 15, 15, 15]cm)
16⅜ (17, 17¾, 18⅜, 20⅞)" (42 [43, 45, 47, 53]cm)

Sage crochet band

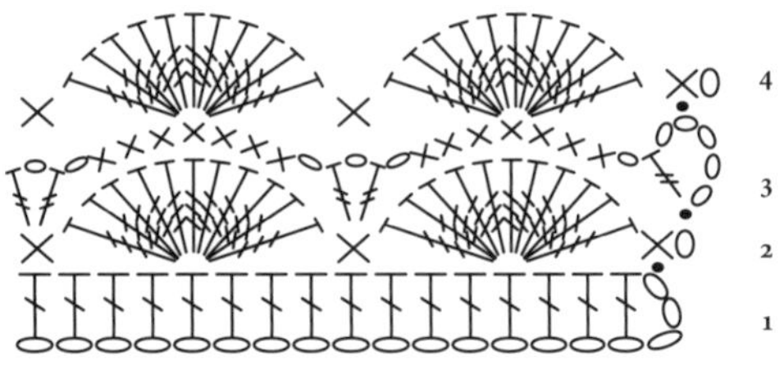
4
3
2
1

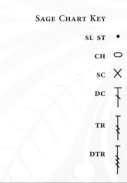

Begin here, then sew this edge to sweater

PATTERN STITCHES

SEED VARIATION (MULT OF 4 STS)

ROW/RND 1 (RS): [K3, p1] around.

ROW/RND 2: K if worked in the rnd, p if worked back and forth.

ROW/RND 3: K all sts.

ROW/RND 4: K if worked in the rnd, p if worked back and forth.

ROW/RND 5: K1, *p1, k3; rep from * across/around, ending with k2.

ROWS/RNDS 6–8: Rep Rows/Rnds 2–4.

Rep Rows/Rnds 1–8 for patt.

1×1 RIB (MULT OF 2 STS)

ROW 1: *K1, p1; rep from * across.

Rep Row 1 for patt.

Crocheted Band

Note: Band is worked in the rnd from upper edge downwards.

Using size 1 crochet hook and pearl cotton, ch 183 (191, 215, 231, 255), join with sl st to beg ch.

RND 1: Ch 2 (counts as 1 dc), dc in ea ch, end with a sl st in top of beg ch-2—184 (192, 216, 232, 256) sts.

RND 2: Ch 1, sc in same space. Work 11 dtr in 4th dc from hook, skip 3 dc, *sc in next dc, skip 3 dc, 11 dtr in next dc, skip 3; rep from * around. Join with sl st in top of beg sc.

RND 3: Ch 5, tr in same space, *ch 1, skip 2 dtr, sc in ea of next 7 dtr, ch 1, (tr, ch 1, tr) in next sc; rep from * around, end ch 1, skip 2 dtr, sc in next 7 dtr, ch 1 and sl st in 4th ch of beg ch.

RND 4: Ch 1, sc into first space of prev rnd, *11 dtr in 4th sc of prev rnd, skip 1 ch-1 space, sc into next ch-1 space; rep from * around, end 11 dtr into 4th sc of prev rnd, sl st into beg sc.

Rep Rnds 3–4 until piece meas 5½" (14cm). Fasten off.

Sage Chart Key

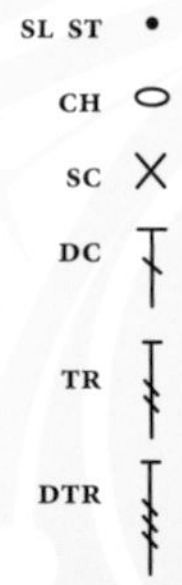
SL ST
CH
SC
DC
TR
DTR

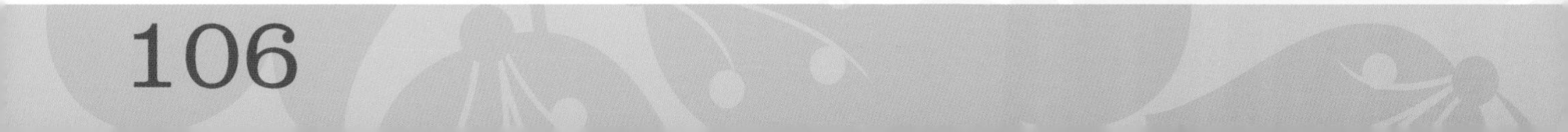

Front and Back

Using size 7 circular needle, CO 152 (160, 176, 192, 208) sts. Place marker and join in a rnd, being careful not to twist the sts. Work in Seed Variation until piece meas 5¼ (5⅝, 5¾, 6¼, 6¼)" (13 [14, 15, 16, 16]cm). Stay in patt throughout.

Armhole Shaping

BO 1 (2, 3, 4, 5) sts, and work across next 75 (78, 85, 92, 97) sts. Join a second ball of yarn and rep across rem sts. From here on, work Front and Back separately at the same time, working back and forth in rows.

NEXT ROW (WS): Rep prev row.

BO 1 st ea end of next 0 (0, 0, 2, 1) rows.

BO 1 st ea end of every 4th row 2 (2, 3, 3, 3) times—70 (72, 76, 78, 84) sts per section.

Work even until pieces meas 11½ (12½, 13, 13⅜, 15)" (29 [32, 33, 34, 38]cm). Cont to work even on Back.

Front Neck

On Front section only: Work across 32 (33, 35, 36, 39) sts, BO 6 (6, 6, 6, 8) sts, join a third ball of yarn to work both sides of Neck at the same time, work to end.

At beg of next 2 rows, BO 2 sts at Neck edge.

BO 1 st at ea Neck edge 8 (8, 8, 9, 10) times—22 (23, 25, 25, 26) sts ea side.

Work even on Front and Back until pieces meas 14¼ (15¼, 15¾, 16¾, 17¾)" (36 [39, 40, 43, 45]cm).

Shoulder Shaping

BO 8 sts at beg of next 2 rows twice.

BO 6 (7, 8, 8, 10) sts ea Shoulder leaving 0 sts on front, and 26 (26, 28, 30, 32) sts on back section. Place these on a holder.

Sleeves

Using size 5 straight needles, CO 68 (70, 72, 76, 86) sts.

Work 5 rows in 1×1 Rib, ending with a RS row.

NEXT ROW (WS): Change to size 7 straight needles and inc 1 st ea end of row 0 (1, 0, 1, 1) times—68 (72, 72, 78, 88) sts.

NEXT ROW (RS): Work Row 1 of Seed Variation, then cont in patt for rest of Sleeve. At the same time, inc 1 st ea end of row every 6th row 3 (2, 4, 2, 3) times—74 (76, 80, 82, 94) sts.

Work even until piece meas 6" (15cm) from beg.

Sleeve Cap

BO 3 sts at beg of next 2 rows 1 (1, 1, 1, 2) times—68 (70, 74, 76, 86) sts.

BO 6 sts at beg of next 2 rows 1 (1, 1, 0, 1) times—56 (58, 62, 76, 70) sts.

BO 4 sts at beg of next 2 rows 3 (3, 3, 2, 1) times—32 (34, 38, 60, 62) sts.

BO 1 st at beg of next 2 rows 0 (0, 5, 10, 12) times—32 (34, 28, 40, 38) sts.

BO 3 sts at beg of next 2 rows 1 (2, 1, 2, 4) times—26 (22, 22, 28, 14) sts.

BO 6 sts at beg of next 2 rows 1 (1, 1, 1, 0) times.

BO rem 14 (10, 10, 16, 14) sts.

Finishing

Weave in ends. Block the knitted pieces. Sew the beg edge of the Crochet Band to bottom edge of Front/Back, easing the knitted section to fit.

Sew the right Shoulder seam. Using size 5 needles and with RS facing and starting at Left Shoulder, pick up and k 42 (42, 42, 42, 46) sts evenly around Front Neck, then pick up the sts on holder for Back Neck.

ROW 1: [K1, p1] across.

ROW 2: BO.

Sew Left Shoulder seam. Sew Sleeves into Armholes. Sew Sleeve seams.

Decorative Tie

Using size 1 crochet hook and pearl cotton, make a chain 28" (71cm) long. Ch 1, turn. Sc in ea ch across. Fasten off. Tie into a bow and tack bow to center front just below the Neckline.

Weave in remaining ends.

MAIDEN'S BLUSH

In a shade reminiscent of a favorite old-fashioned rose, this delightful shrug features a combination of smooth linen and textured cotton. (All-cotton "fun" yarns are scarce, so I felt compelled to dream up a sweater design for this cotton eyelash yarn when I found it.) The linen color shows through the eyelash yarn on the bodice, creating a tone-on-tone tweed. Using two yarns of different fibers held together is one way to create your own custom blend of fibers.

SKILL LEVEL
Experienced

METHOD
Knit

SIZES
To fit actual bust size: 34 (36, 39)" (86 [91, 99]cm)

FINISHED MEASUREMENTS
Bust: Approx 37½ (39, 42¾)" (95 [99, 109]cm)

YARN
2 (2, 3) (1¾ oz./50g, 170 yd./155m) mini cones lace weight eyelash yarn (A)

3 (4, 4) (3½ oz./100g, 270 yd./247m) skeins sport weight yarn (B)

NEEDLES
Size US 6 (4mm) straight needles

40" (100cm) size US 5 (3.75mm) circular needle

If necessary, change needle size to obtain correct gauge.

NOTIONS
Yarn needle

GAUGE
18 sts and 28 rows = 4" (10cm) in St st with both yarns held tog on size US 6 (4mm) needles

The project shown at right was made using Halcyon Casco Bay Cotton Eyelash (100% cotton, 1¾ oz./50g, 170 yd./155m) in color 206 (A) and Louet Euroflax Fine/Sport Weight (100% linen, 3½ oz./100g, 270 yd./247m) in Soft Coral (B).

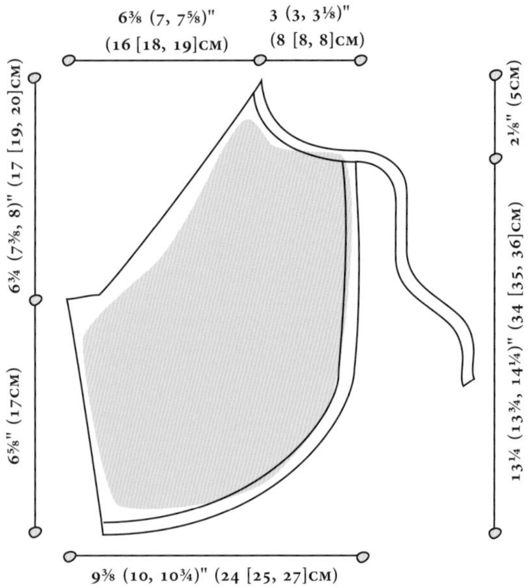
6⅜ (7, 7⅝)" (16 [18, 19]cm)
3 (3, 3⅛)" (8 [8, 8]cm)
6¾ (7⅞, 8)" (17 [19, 20]cm)
6⅝" (17cm)
2⅛" (5cm)
13¼ (13¾, 14¼)" (34 [35, 36]cm)
9⅜ (10, 10¾)" (24 [25, 27]cm)

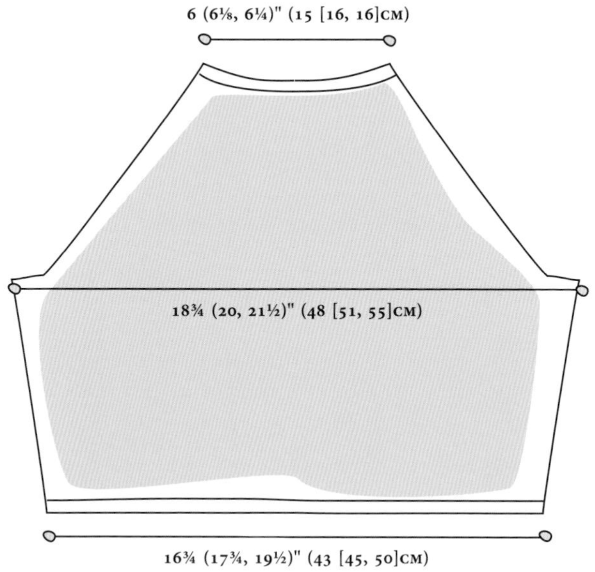
6 (6⅛, 6¼)" (15 [16, 16]cm)
18¾ (20, 21½)" (48 [51, 55]cm)
16¾ (17¾, 19½)" (43 [45, 50]cm)

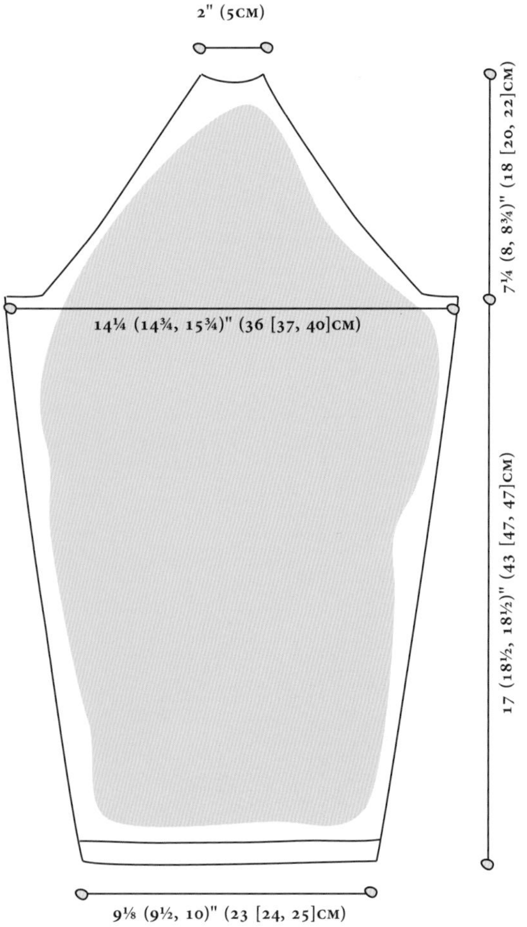
2" (5cm)
14¼ (14¾, 15¾)" (36 [37, 40]cm)
7¼ (8, 8¾)" (18 [20, 22]cm)
17 (18½, 18½)" (43 [47, 47]cm)
9⅛ (9½, 10)" (23 [24, 25]cm)

PATTERN STITCH

LACE (MULT OF 5 STS)

ROW 1 (RS): K all sts.

ROW 2: P all sts.

ROW 3: K1, *yo, sl1, k2tog, psso, yo, k2; rep from * to last st, k1.

ROW 4: P all sts.

Rep Rows 1–4 for patt.

Right Front

Using size 6 needles and with 1 strand of ea of the yarns held tog, CO 17 (19, 21) sts. Work in St st throughout.

Front Opening

Note: Work Side Shaping on the foll rows as well.

ROW 1 (RS): K all sts.

ROW 2 AND ALL WS ROWS: P all sts.

ROW 3: CO 4 (4, 5) sts, work to end.

ROW 5: CO 3 (3, 4) sts, work to end.

ROW 7: CO 3 (3, 3) sts, work to end.

ROW 9: CO 2 (2, 2) sts, work to end.

Cont shaping, inc 1 st at beg of ea RS row 9 times.

Side Shaping

AT THE SAME TIME: Inc 1 st every 6th row 4 times at end of row.

Raglan Shaping

When piece meas 6⅝" (17cm) and sts total 42 (44, 48), beg Raglan Shaping.

BO 3 at beg of next WS row. Then, dec 1 st at beg of ea WS row until there are 16 (18, 23) sts. Piece meas 11½ (12, 12)" (29 [30, 30]cm).

Neck Opening

Cont Raglan Shaping at Armhole edge, and, AT THE SAME TIME, shape the Neck opening. At beg of next RS row, BO 5 sts. At beg of next RS row, [BO 2 sts] twice. At beg of next RS row, [BO 1 st] 4 times.

When 2 (3, 6) sts rem, BO all sts.

Left Front

Work as for Right Front, reversing shaping. K 1 row, then beg the Front opening shaping on the p row (WS).

Back

Using size 6 needles and with both yarns held tog, CO 76 (82, 88) sts. At ea side edge, inc 1 st every 6th row 4 times—84 (92, 96) sts.

When piece meas 6⅝" (17cm), beg Raglan Shaping same as for Fronts, making the dec at beg of ea row until 30 (32, 32) sts rem. BO all sts.

Sleeves

Using size 6 needles and with both yarns held tog, CO 60 sts.

ROW 1: [K1, p1] across. Cut eyelash yarn, and cont with sport weight yarn only.

ROW 2 (RS): [K1, k2tog] across—40 sts.

ROW 3: P all sts.

ROW 4: Work Row 1 of Lace patt. Cont to work in Lace patt, staying in patt throughout.

Work even for 1" (3cm). Then inc 1 st at ea side edge every 6th row 12 (13, 15) times—64 (66, 70) sts. Work even until Sleeve meas 17 (18½, 18½)" (43 [47, 47]cm).

Raglan Shaping

BO 2 (2, 3) sts at beg of next two rows. BO 1 st at beg of ea row until 11 sts rem. BO all sts.

Finishing

Weave in ends. Block pieces. Sew side seams of Bodice. Sew Sleeve seams. Sew Sleeves into Armholes, easing if necessary.

Bodice Edging

Using size 5 circular needle and yarn B, beg at top of one Bodice Front opening with RS facing and pick up and k 4 sts per 1" (3cm) foll the curve of the Bodice. At the bottom where the edge is straight, [pick up 3 sts, skip 1] across. Cont up to the curve of the Front Bodice, then pick up 4 sts per 1" (3cm) to top.

ROW 1 (WS): P all sts.

ROW 2: [K1, p1] across.

ROW 3: BO kwise loosely.

Neck Edging and Ties

Using size 5 circular needle and sport weight yarn, CO 56 sts. Working continuously and with RS facing, beg along top of the Bodice Edging and pick up and k 4 sts per 1" (3cm) along tops of edging, upper edge of Bodice, Sleeve, Back, other Bodice section, and the top of the Bodice Edging. CO 56 sts. Work same as for Rows 1–3 of Bodice Edging.

Weave in remaining ends.

TRAVELING VINE

Waist-shaped and shirt-tailed, this cool cotton summer top features an easy-to-knit lace panel in front and back, and short-row shaping of the cap sleeves. This design shows one way that two yarns of differing gauges can be combined in one garment.

SKILL LEVEL
Intermediate

METHOD
Knit and Crochet

SIZES
To fit actual bust/waist size: 34/26 (36/28, 39/31, 42/34, 44/37)" (86/66 [91/71, 99/79, 107/86, 112/94]cm)

FINISHED MEASUREMENTS
Bust/Waist: Approx 39/33 (41/36, 44/39, 46/41, 49/45)" (99/84 [104/91, 112/99, 117/104, 124/114]cm)

YARN
6 (6, 7, 7, 8) (1¾ oz./50g, 83 yd./76m) skeins worsted weight yarn (A)

3 (3, 3, 4, 4) (3½ oz./100g, 196 yd./180m) skeins variegated worsted weight yarn (B)

NEEDLES
Size US 3 (3.25mm) straight needles

Size US 5 (3.75mm straight needles

Size US 6 (4mm) straight needles

Size US 8 (5mm) straight needles

If necessary, change needle size to obtain correct gauge.

HOOK
Size US E/4 (3.5mm) crochet hook

NOTIONS
Yarn needle

GAUGE
17 sts and 24 rows = 4" (10cm) in St st using yarn A and size US 6 (4mm) needles

20 sts and 28 rows = 4" (10cm) in St st using yarn B and size US 5 (3.75mm) needles

Lace Panel = 8" (20cm) wide using yarn B and size US 3 (3.25mm) needles

The project shown at right was made using Knit One, Crochet Too Cotonade (100% cotton, 1¾ oz./50g, 83 yd./76m) in color 631 Periwinkle (A) and Knit One, Crochet Too Ty-Dy (100% cotton, 3½ oz./100g, 196 yd./180m) in Blue Pansy (B).

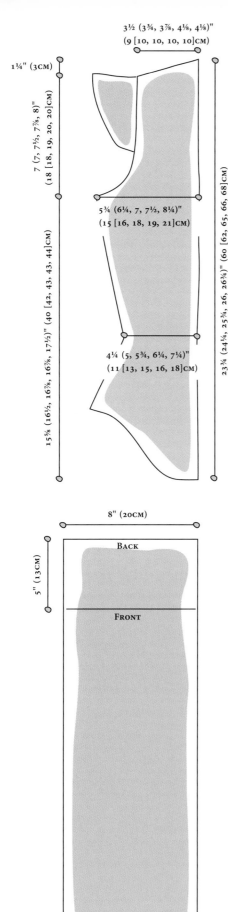

3½ (3¾, 3⅞, 4⅛, 4⅛)"
(9 [10, 10, 10, 10]CM)

1¼" (3CM)

7 (7, 7½, 7⅞, 8)"
(18 [18, 19, 20, 20]CM)

5¾ (6¼, 7, 7½, 8¼)"
(15 [16, 18, 19, 21]CM)

23¾ (24¼, 25¾, 26, 26¾)" (60 [62, 65, 66, 68]CM)

15⅝ (16½, 16⅞, 16⅞, 17½)" (40 [42, 43, 43, 44]CM)

4¼ (5, 5¾, 6¼, 7¼)"
(11 [13, 15, 16, 18]CM)

8" (20CM)

5" (13CM)

BACK

FRONT

ABBREVIATIONS

KB1

Knit into the back instead of the front of a st.

K2TOG TBL

Knit 2 sts tog through the back loops.

P2TOG TBL

Purl 2 sts tog through the back loops.

PATTERN STITCHES

TRAVELING VINE LACE (MULT OF 8 + 4 STS)

ROW 1 (RS): K2, *yo, kb1, yo, k2tog tbl, k5; rep from * across, end k2.

ROW 2: P2, *p4, p2tog tbl, p3; rep from * across, end p2.

ROW 3: K2, *yo, kb1, yo, k2, k2tog tbl, k3; rep from * across, end k2.

ROW 4: P2, *p2, p2tog tbl, p5; rep from * across, end p2.

ROW 5: K2, *kb1, yo, k4, k2tog tbl, k1, yo; rep from * across, end k2.

ROW 6: P2, *p1, p2tog tbl, p6; rep from * across, end p2.

ROW 7: K2, *k5, k2tog, yo, kb1, yo; rep from * across, end k2.

ROW 8: P2, *p3, p2tog, p4; rep from * across, end p2.

ROW 9: K2, *k3, k2tog, k2, yo, kb1, yo; rep from * across, end k2.

ROW 10: P2, *p5, p2tog, p2; rep from * across, end p2.

ROW 11: K2, *yo, k1, k2tog, k4, yo, kb1; rep from * across, end k2.

ROW 12: P2, *p6, p2tog, p1; rep from * across, end p2.

Rep Rows 1–12 for patt.

Back Lace Panel

Using size 3 needles and yarn B, CO 44 sts and work Traveling Vine Lace until piece meas approx 23¾ (24¼, 25¾, 26, 26¾)" (60 [62, 65, 66, 68]cm). BO all sts after Row 12 of patt.

Front Lace Panel

Using size 3 needles and yarn B, CO 44 sts and work Traveling Vine Lace until piece meas approx 18¾ (19¼, 20¾, 21, 21¾)" (48 [49, 53, 53, 55]cm). BO all sts after Row 12 of patt.

Right Front Side Panel
Using size 6 needles and yarn A, CO 9 (12, 15, 18, 22) sts. K 1 row.

Shirttail Edge
CO 2 sts at beg of next WS row.

CO 1 st at beg of next 9 WS rows.

CO 2 sts at beg of next WS row.

CO 3 sts at beg of next WS row—25 (28, 31, 34, 38) sts.

Work 4 rows even.

Dec 1 st at left edge every other row 7 times—18 (21, 24, 27, 31) sts.

Work even until piece meas 8 (9⅛, 9⅛, 9½, 11⅛)" (20 [23, 23, 24, 28]cm).

Inc 1 st at left edge every 6th row 7 (6, 6, 5, 4) times—25 (27, 30, 32, 35) sts.

Work even until piece meas 15⅝ (16½, 16⅞, 16⅞, 17½)" (40 [42, 42, 42, 44]cm).

Armhole Shaping
BO 2 (3, 3, 4, 5) sts at beg of next WS row.

BO 2 (2, 2, 2, 3) sts at beg of next WS row.

BO 2 sts at beg of next WS row.

BO 1 st at beg of next WS row 3 (3, 4, 5, 5) times—16 (17, 19, 19, 20) sts.

Work even until Armhole meas 7 (7, 7½, 7⅞, 8)" (18 [18, 19, 19, 20]cm).

Shoulder Shaping
BO 5 sts at beg of next WS row 3 times.

BO 1 (2, 4, 4, 5) rem sts.

Left Front Side Panel
Using size 6 needles and yarn A, CO 9 (12, 15, 18, 22) sts. Foll instructions for Right Front, reversing all shaping (work shaping at beg of RS rows).

Back Side Panels
Rep instructions for Right and Left Front Side Panels.

Sleeves
Sew Shoulder seams. Using size 5 needles and yarn B, with RS facing and beg 5½ (5½, 5¾, 6, 6)" (14 [14, 15, 15, 15]cm) from the Shoulder seam, pick up and k along the Armhole edge 27 (27, 29, 30, 30) sts from one side panel, then the same number of sts and same distance along the other side panel.

ROW 1 (WS): P all sts.

ROW 2: K2tog, k to 3 sts from the end, w&t. P up to 3 sts from other end, w&t, k to end of row, k2tog.

ROW 3: P2tog, p to last 2 sts, p2tog.

Rep Rows 2–3 5 times. BO 3 sts at beg of next 2 rows 3 times, then BO rem sts.

Finishing
Weave in ends. Block ea piece. Sew Front Lace Panel to the two Front Side Panels, lining them up at the lower edges. Sew Back Lace Panel to the two Back Side Panels, lining them up at both top and bottom edges. Sew side seams.

Neck Trim
Using crochet hook and yarn B, starting at one Shoulder, sc around Neck as folls: Work evenly along yarn A sections, skip every 3rd st across the Lace Panels, and dec 2 sts at Front corners. At end of rnd, sl st into beg sc, ch 1. Work a second rnd, dec 2 sts at front corners as before, and across Front Lace Panel only work as foll: *sc in sc twice, make picot: ch 2, sl st into 1st ch; rep from *. Fasten to beg sc, fasten off.

Ties (make 2)
Using crochet hook and yarn B, ch 60, ch 1 to turn, and sl st in ea ch to beg. Fasten off.

Fasten a Tie to ea side of the Front Lace Panel on the back of the panel, then using the crochet hook to pull the Ties through the sts, weave through the row of sc at the top of the Lace Panel to the center and tie a bow.

Bottom Edging
Using crochet hook and yarn A, sc along bottom edges beg and ending at ea Lace Panel (do not work across panels).

Armhole/Cap Sleeve Edging
Using crochet hook and yarn A, sc along lower part of Armhole beg and ending at edges of Cap Sleeve. Using yarn B, fasten onto one end of Cap Sleeve and work picot (same as earlier) along edge of Sleeve.

Weave in remaining ends.

OLIVE IN FLOWER

A summer tank to wear everywhere … and in soft organic color-grown cotton, you will want to!

SKILL LEVEL	SIZES	YARN	NEEDLES	NOTIONS	GAUGE
Advanced Beginner	To fit actual bust size: 32 (34½, 37, 40, 42½, 46)" (81 [88, 94, 102, 108, 117]cm).	6 (6, 7, 7, 9, 10) (1¾ oz./50g, 88 yd./81m) skeins worsted weight yarn, 5 (5, 6, 6, 7, 8) skeins MC, 1 (1, 1, 1, 2, 2) skeins CC	32" (80cm) (smaller sizes) or 40" (100cm) (larger sizes) size US 5 (3.75mm) circular needle	Stitch marker Yarn needle	18 sts and 24 rows = 4" (10cm) in patt on size US 6 (4mm) needles
METHOD Knit	*The tank is sized to fit closely. For a looser fit, choose a size larger than your usual size.*		32" (80cm) or 40" (100cm) size US 6 (4mm) circular needle		
	FINISHED MEASUREMENTS Approx same as Sizes		*If necessary, change needle size to obtain correct gauge.*		

The project shown at right was made using Ecobutterfly Pakucho (100% certified organic cotton, 1¾ oz./50g, 88 yd./81m) in Sage (MC) and Natural (CC).

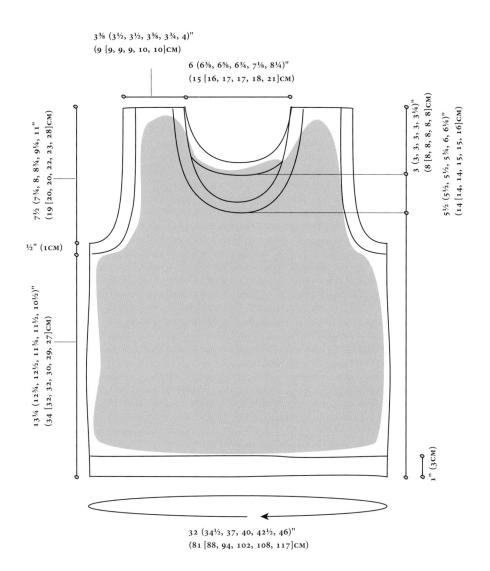

3⅜ (3½, 3½, 3⅝, 3¾, 4)"
(9 [9, 9, 9, 10, 10]CM)

6 (6⅜, 6⅝, 6¾, 7⅛, 8¼)"
(15 [16, 17, 17, 18, 21]CM)

3 (3, 3, 3, 3, 3¼)"
(8 [8, 8, 8, 8, 8]CM)

5½ (5½, 5½, 5¾, 6, 6¼)"
(14 [14, 14, 15, 15, 16]CM)

7½ (7¾, 8, 8¾, 9¼, 11)"
(19 [20, 20, 22, 23, 28]CM)

½" (1CM)

13¼ (12¾, 12½, 11¾, 11½, 10½)"
(34 [32, 32, 30, 29, 27]CM)

1" (3CM)

32 (34½, 37, 40, 42½, 46)"
(81 [88, 94, 102, 108, 117]CM)

PATTERN STITCHES

SEED VARIATION 2 (MULT OF 4 STS)

ROW/RND 1: [K1, p1] across/around.

ROW/RND 2 (RS): K all sts.

ROW/RND 3: [P1, k1] across/around.

ROW/RND 4: K all sts.

Rep Rows/Rnds 1–4 for patt.

DIAGONAL SEED (MULT OF 6 STS)

ROW/RND 1 (RS): [K5, p1] across/around.

ROW/RND 2 AND ALL EVEN ROWS: P if working back and forth, k if working in rnd.

ROW/RND 3: P1, *k5, p1; rep from * ending k5.

ROW/RND 5: K1, *p1, k5; rep from * ending p1, k4.

ROW/RND 7: K2, *p1, k5; rep from * ending p1, k3.

ROW/RND 9: K3, *p1, k5; rep from * ending p1, k2.

ROW/RND 11: K4, *p1, k5; rep from * ending p1, k1.

Rep Rows/Rnds 1–11 for patt.

Body

Using size 5 circular needle and CC, CO 132 (140, 152, 164, 172, 184) sts. Place marker and join in a rnd, being careful not to twist the sts. Work Rnds 1–4 of Seed Variation 2 twice (8 rnds). Break off CC.

Note: Slip marker on each rnd.

NEXT RND: Change to size 6 circular needles and MC. P and inc 12 (16, 16, 16, 20, 20) sts evenly spaced on first rnd—144 (156, 168, 180, 192, 204) sts.

NEXT RND: Beg Diagonal Seed, and cont in patt until piece meas 13¼ (12¾, 12½, 11¾, 11½, 10½)" (34 [32, 32, 30, 29, 27]cm) from beg.

Divide for Front and Back

Armhole Shaping

Staying in Diagonal Seed throughout, remove marker, BO 3 (4, 5, 5, 7, 8) sts for Armhole, work across next 69 (74, 79, 85, 89, 94) sts (Front). Join a second ball of yarn and BO 3 (4, 5, 5,

7, 8) sts for second Armhole and work across next 69 (74, 79, 85, 89, 94) sts (Back). Turn.

NEXT ROW (WS): Rep BO at beg of Back and beg of Front—66 (70, 74, 80, 82, 86) sts on ea.

From here on, work Front and Back at same time, working back and forth on the circular needle. Cont to shape Armholes: BO 1 st at ea end of every row 3 (3, 3, 4, 4, 4) times—60 (64, 68, 72, 74, 78) sts on ea of Front and Back.

BO 1 st ea end of every RS row 3 (4, 4, 5, 6, 6) times—54 (56, 60, 62, 62, 66) sts.

When piece meas 15½ (15½, 15½, 15¼, 15¼, 15¾)" (39 [39, 39, 39, 39, 40]cm) and Armholes meas 2¼ (2¾, 3, 3½, 3¾, 5¼)" (6 [7, 8, 9, 9, 13]cm) cont to work even on the Back, and beg shaping Front Neck.

Front Neck
NEXT ROW (RS): Work across 23 (23, 25, 26, 25, 27) sts, join a third ball of yarn and BO 8 (10, 10, 10, 12, 12) sts at the center, work to end of row.

At Front Neck edges:
BO 2 (2, 3, 3, 2, 2) sts at beg of next 2 rows.

BO 1 st at beg of every row 3 times.

BO 1 st at ea end of every RS row 6 (6, 7, 7, 7, 9) times—12 (12, 12, 13, 13, 13) sts ea side of Neck. Cont to work even on these sts.

Back Neck
When pieces meas 18 (18, 18, 18, 18¼, 18¼)" (46 [46, 46, 46, 46, 46]cm) from beg, ending with a WS row, shape Back Neck.

NEXT ROW (RS): Work across 22 (22, 24, 25, 25, 26) sts, join a 4th ball of yarn and BO center 10 (12, 12, 12, 12, 14) sts, work to end of row.

At Back Neck edges:
BO 3 (3, 5, 5, 5, 5) sts at beg of next 2 rows.

BO 1 st at ea end of every RS row 7 (7, 7, 7, 7, 8) times.

Shoulder Shaping
When pieces meas 21 (21, 21, 21, 21¼, 22)" (53 [53, 53, 53, 54, 56]cm) from beg, BO rem 12 (12, 12, 13, 13, 13) sts at ea Shoulder.

Finishing

Armhole Bands
Weave in ends. Block pieces if needed. Using size 5 needles (work back and forth on circular, or change to straight needles) and CC, beg at top of one Armhole with RS facing, pick up and k 36 (40, 42, 46, 50, 56) sts evenly along Front, and the same number along Back—72 (80, 84, 92, 100, 112) sts. Work Rows 1–4 of Seed Variation 2.

NEXT ROW (WS): Cut CC, join MC and BO kwise (giving a two-tone effect on the RS of the edging.) Rep for second Armhole Band, picking up sts along Back first, then Front.

Sew one Shoulder.

Neck Band
Using size 5 needles (work back and forth on circular, or change to straight needles) and CC, and with RS facing, pick up and k 108 (112, 112, 116, 120, 128) sts evenly along entire Neck edge starting at open Shoulder. Work Rows 1–4 of Seed Variation 2.

NEXT ROW (WS): Cut CC, join MC and BO kwise.

Sew rem Shoulder.

Bottom Band Edging
Using size 5 circular needle and CC, with WS facing, pick up and k 1 st for ea st of edge—132 (140, 152, 164, 172, 184) sts.

BO. Weave in remaining ends.

WILD OATS

Created of hard-wearing hemp, this lace and cable purse is ready to go places. The zippered top holds items securely inside, and a contrasting lining shows off the knitted pattern stitches.

SKILL LEVEL	FINISHED MEASUREMENTS	YARN	NEEDLES	NOTIONS	GAUGE
Intermediate	Approx 12" × 10" (30cm × 25cm)	1 (16 oz./450g, 425 yd./392m) cone worsted weight yarn	Size US 6 (4mm) straight needles	Cable needle	12 sts and 24 rows = 4" (10cm) in garter st on size US 10 (6mm) needles
METHOD			Size US 10 (6mm) straight needles	Yarn needle	
Knit				4 1" (3cm) D-rings	
			If necessary, change needle size to obtain correct gauge.	12" (30cm) zipper	
SIZE				½ yd. (.5m) contrasting fabric for lining	
One size				Sewing needle	
				Pins	
				Thread to match yarn	

The project shown at right was made using Lanaknits Hemp12, (100% hemp, 16 oz./450g, 425 yd./392m) in Natural. This project only uses a portion of the yarn on the cone. I suggest using the remaining yarn to create a matching accessory, such as Silver Saxifrage on page 56.

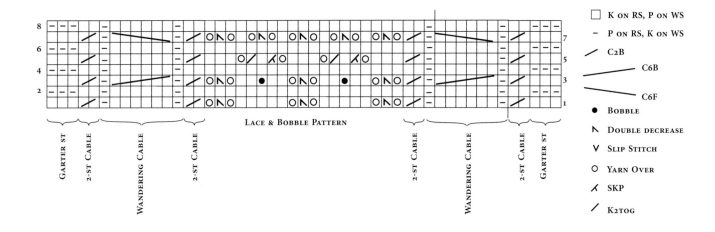

LACE & BOBBLE PATTERN

GARTER ST | 2-ST CABLE | WANDERING CABLE | 2-ST CABLE | 2-ST CABLE | WANDERING CABLE | 2-ST CABLE | GARTER ST

☐ K on RS, P on WS
– P on RS, K on WS
╱ C2B
⟍ C6B
╱ C6F
● Bobble
⋀ Double decrease
V Slip Stitch
O Yarn Over
ᐟ SKP
╱ K2tog

ABBREVIATIONS

C6B
Slip 3 sts to cn and hold to back, k3, k3 from cn.

C6F
Slip 3 sts to cn and hold to front, k3, k3 from cn.

C2B
Slip 1 st to cn and hold to back, k1, k1 from cn.

B
Bobble.

DD
Double decrease.

PATTERN STITCHES

2-ST CABLE (WORKED OVER 2 STS)
ROW 1 (RS): C2B.
ROW 2: P all sts.
Rep Rows 1–2 for patt.

WANDERING CABLE (WORKED OVER 8 STS)
ROW 1 (RS): P1, k6, p1.
ROW 2 AND ALL WS ROWS: K1, p6, k1.
ROW 3: P1, C6B, p1.
ROW 5: P1, k6, p1.
ROW 7: P1, C6F, p1.
Rep Rows 1–8 for patt.

LACE & BOBBLE (WORKED OVER 19 STS)
ROW 1 (RS): [Yo, dd, yo, k5] twice, end yo, dd, yo.
ROW 2 (AND ALL WS ROWS): P all sts.
ROW 3: [Yo, dd, yo, k2, B, k2] twice, end yo, dd, yo.
ROW 5: [K3, yo, SKP, k1, k2tog, yo] twice, end k3.
ROW 7: [Yo, dd, yo, k1] four times, end yo, dd, yo.

BOBBLE
K into front, back, and front of next stitch, turn and p, turn and k, turn and p, then slip 2nd st over first, then 3rd st over first, and place rem st on right needle.

DOUBLE DECREASE
K2tog through backs of loops, slip stitch on left needle, pass foll st over, then place st back on right needle.

Purse Side (Make 2)
Using size 10 needles, CO 18 sts. Work in garter st.

ROWS 1, 3, 5 AND 7 (RS): Inc 6 sts evenly spaced across row.

ROW 2 (AND ALL WS ROWS): K all sts.

ROW 9: Inc 7 sts evenly spaced across row – 49 sts.

ROWS 10–14: K all sts.

Work Rows 1–8 of chart 5 times. Work 6 rows in garter st. BO.

Finishing
Sew the two halves tog along sides and bottom edges.

Tabs for D-Rings
Using size 6 needles, pick up and k 6 sts (working into the bumps of the garter st) directly above a Wandering Cable on one Purse Side. K 12 rows in St st, BO and cut end, leaving a long tail of yarn to sew the end to the purse. Rep above rem cable on same Purse Side, then rep for other Purse Side. Slip a D-Ring on ea tab, and sew tab through all layers along the pick up and k row.

Handle (make 2)
Using size 6 needles, CO 6 sts and work in St st for 24" (61cm). BO and cut end leaving 30" (76cm) tail to sew the Handle. With the same Handle end, fold 1½" (4cm) from the end and place the fold over a D-ring. Sew the end to the Handle, then bring the sides of the Handle tog to form a tube and sew up to within 3" (8cm) of the opposite end. Fold the end and sew over the D-ring on same side of Purse.

Sew second Handle to D-rings on opposite side of Purse.

Pin one side of zipper to inside of Purse with top edge of purse next to zipper teeth. Rep for other side of zipper. Hand sew along zipper tapes. Finish ends to neatly align with side seams and with zipper tape ends inside the Purse.

Lining
Cut out lining fabric ½" (1cm) larger than Purse all around. Machine sew the side and bottom seams using a ½" (1cm) seam allowance. Do not turn. Press the upper edge ½" (1cm) to WS and place lining inside purse. Pin lining to zipper tape, aligning with prev stitching. Sew lining to zipper tape by hand using needle and sewing thread.

AUTUMN OAK LEAF

A small purse the color of bronzed autumn leaves is a perfect accessory for snazzy occasions, and a great project for a glossy rayon yarn. This yarn is easier to crochet than to knit because the yarn is slippery and its plies can flatten out on a knitting needle, but this isn't a problem with crochet. To substitute a different yarn, choose one that is compatible with a size D crochet hook.

SKILL LEVEL
Beginner

METHOD
Crochet

SIZE
One size

FINISHED MEASUREMENTS
Approx 10" × 8½" (25cm × 22cm)

YARN
1 (7½ oz./215g, 1110 yd./1000m) cone fingering weight yarn

HOOK
Size US D/3 (3.25mm) crochet hook

If necessary, change hook size to obtain correct gauge.

NOTIONS
Stitch marker

Yarn needle

Dental floss threader

1¼ oz. (35g) box 8/0 seed beads

5¼" × 3½" (13cm × 9cm) pair of Lucite handles with sewing holes

GAUGE
20 sc or dc = 4" (10cm)

The project shown at right was made using Valley Yarns Susi Rayon (100% rayon, 7½ oz./215g, 1110 yd./1000m) in color 7404 Golden Brown

The project shown at right was made using Dyna-Mites in Iris Purple.

The project shown at right was made using handles from Lacis.

PATTERN STITCHES

BEADED SC
Before working sc, slide a bead up to the hook, then sc in appropriate st.

PREPARATION
Wind off approx half of the yarn onto another object such as an empty cone, or a piece of cardboard about 2" × 6" (5cm × 15cm). (Yarns made from fibers other than rayon can be wound into a ball.) Bring the two ends together and place the threader onto the doubled yarn. Thread the seed beads onto the yarn, using the entire box of beads. As you crochet, carefully reel off several yards of the yarn at a time and slide the beads along.

Purse
Using a size D/3 crochet hook and 2 beaded strands of yarn held tog, make a chain 6" (15cm) long.

RND 1: Ch 1 to turn, and sc in ea ch across. Work 3 sc in the last ch, then sc along the opposite side. Work 3 sc in the last ch.

RND 2: Working in a continuous rnd without joining to last st with a sl st at the end, inc 4 sts evenly spaced along ea side of the piece, and work 3 sc in ea end st—14 sts inc.

RNDS 3–6: Rep Rnd 2. End these four rnds after the final 3 sc made in the end st. From here, join end of ea rnd with a sl st.

The foll rnds are worked in the rnd, but the sc rnds are worked on the WS—this is so the beads will appear on the RS of the purse.

RND 7 (RS): Ch 2 (counts as 1 dc), dc in ea sc around. Fasten to top of beg ch-2.

RND 8 (WS): Ch 1, turn, and sc on top of ending dc of prev rnd. *Beaded sc in next dc, sc in next dc; rep from * around, ending with a sl st in beg sc. Make sure to end with a beaded sc, adding a st if needed, to keep in the pattern of beaded sc foll by a plain sc.

RND 9: Ch 2, turn, and dc in ea sc around, ending with a sl st into top of beg ch2.

Rep Rnds 8–9 until piece meas approx 7" (18cm) above the bottom and there are 12 beaded rnds. End after a dc rnd.

Edging
RND 1: Ch 1 and sc in dc, *ch 2, skip 1 dc, sc in next dc; rep from * around, end ch 2, sl st into top of beg sc.

RND 2: Sl st into first ch-2 sp, ch 2 (counts as 1 dc), 2 dc into ch-2 sp, *3 dc in next ch-2 sp; rep from * around. Join with sl st to top of beg ch-2.

RND 3: Ch 1 and turn. In ea 3 dc group work: beaded sc in first dc, (sc, ch 3, sc) in next dc, beaded sc in third dc. Join to top of beg beaded sc and fasten off.

Finishing

Attach Handles
Thread needle with a 1 yd. (1m) length of two strands of yarn held tog. Stitching along the bottom of Rnd 2 of Edging, align the center sewing hole of the handle with the WS of the center front of the Purse (either side of the Purse can be the front). Sew the handle to the Purse while lightly gathering the Purse fabric with ea stitch (grab more fabric than needed into ea st), working from the center outwards. Work from one hole to the next (stitch along, not around the handle) so the sts form a horizontal line along the inside of the handle. For extra security, st twice at ea st placement. When you reach the end of the holes, work the needle through the sts back to the center hole and proceed in the other direction. Fasten the other handle onto the back of the Purse the same way, making sure the handles line up.

Tie
With two strands of yarn held tog, make a chain 45" (114cm) long. Turn, sc along ch to beg, then fasten off. Thread the yarn needle with a short length of yarn, sew through one end of the Tie and knot the yarn. Use the needle to thread the Tie through the top row of dc (just beneath the first Edging Rnd) beg at the front center. Draw up the Tie and adjust until the bag is slightly gathered and yet open enough for the inside of the purse to be accessible. Tie a bow.

Weave in ends.

COTTON BOLL

Finally, a knitted hat with elegance! Wear this classy pillbox for fluffy, fashionable warmth. Who could ask for more? A hat made of such beautiful yarn is a treasure—treat it well and it could become a family heirloom. The cabled band is knitted and the crown of the hat is crocheted.

SKILL LEVEL
Intermediate

METHOD
Knit and Crochet

SIZE
One size

FINISHED MEASUREMENTS
Approx 22–23" (56–58cm) head circumference

YARN
2 (1¾ oz./50g, 41 yd./37m) skeins chunky weight yarn (A)

1 (1¾ oz./50g, 88 yd./80m) skein worsted weight yarn (B)

NEEDLES
Size US 11 (8mm) straight needles

32" (80cm) size US 11 (8mm) circular needle

If necessary, change needle size to obtain correct gauge.

HOOK
Size US F/5 (3.75mm) crochet hook

NOTIONS
Cable needle

Yarn needle

GAUGE
9 sts and 14 rows = 4" (10cm) in St st

The project shown at right was made using Ecobutterfly Monarch (100% certified organic artisan cotton, 1¾ oz./50g, 41 yd./37m) in Marshmallow (A) and Ecobutterfly Pakucho (100% certified organic cotton, 1¾ oz./50g, 88 yd./80m) in Natural (B).

C6B

Slip 3 sts to cn and hold in back, k3, k3 from cn.

C6F

Slip 3 sts to cn and hold in front, k3, k3 from cn.

PATTERN STITCH

REVERSE STOCKINETTE STITCH (MULT OF 1 ST)

ROW 1 (RS): P all sts.

ROW 2: K all sts.

Rep Rows 1–2 for patt.

Cabled Band

Using size 11 straight needles and with yarn A, CO 12 sts.

ROW 1 (RS): K all sts.

ROWS 2, 4, 6 AND 8: P all sts.

ROW 3: [C6B] twice.

ROW 5: K all sts.

ROW 7: K3, C6F, k3.

Rep Rows 1–8 until the Band is the desired length, approx 22–23" (56–58cm), ending after Row 8 of patt. Try the Band around your head and check that the ends meet comfortably without stretching. BO.

Edging

Using size 11 circular needles and with RS of Cabled Band facing, pick up and k 3 sts along ea beg 2 rows, 4 sts along ea curve that was created by the Row 3 cables, and 1 st at ea ending p row (Row 8 of patt).

ROW 1 (RS): K all sts.

ROW 2: P all sts.

Cont to work in Reverse Stockinette Stitch for 7 rows. BO. Rep on opposite edge of Cabled Band.

Finishing

Sew ends of Band tog to form a tube. Roll/coil ea Edging to the WS and loosely sew to the inside edge of the Cabled Band.

Crocheted Crown

With the size F/5 crochet hook and yarn B, ch 3. Sl st into the beg ch to form a ring. Ch 1 and work 6 sc in the ring. Join with a sl st into the beg sc of the rnd.

NEXT RND: Ch 1, sc into the same space. [2 sc into next st, sc] rep around. Join to top of beg sc. Rep this rnd 4 times.

NEXT RND: Sc in ea st around, inc (by making 2 sc in one st) several times as needed to keep piece flat. Cont in this manner until the circle fits the top of the hat brim. Check this by placing its edges along the seam of the rolled edge, and securing in several places with pins. Make sure the top fits loosely so that it will have to be eased as it is sewn in. When the top is the correct size, sew it loosely to the seam of the rolled edge. With a hairbrush, lightly brush the rolled edging to fluff.

Weave in ends.

DARK RASPBERRY

A one-skein project in hemp, this easy-care, easy-wear kerchief features a simple lace pattern. Wear it as a head scarf, draped over a shoulder, or around the upper hip—the knitted mesh is shape-conforming. This project can be made shawl-size: buy extra skeins of yarn and use a longer circular needle as the piece grows.

SKILL LEVEL
Beginner

METHOD
Knit

SIZE
One size

FINISHED MEASUREMENTS
Approx 40" × 13" (102cm × 33cm) relaxed. Stretches to about 22" (56cm) deep.

YARN
1 (3½ oz./100g, 165 yd./151m) skein sport weight yarn

NEEDLES
Size US 1 (2.25mm) straight needles

32" (80cm) or longer size US 1 (2.25mm) circular needles

If necessary, change needle size to obtain correct gauge.

HOOK
Size US D/3 (3.25mm) crochet hook

NOTIONS
Scrap cardboard

Yarn needle

GAUGE
Not important for this project

The project shown above was made using Lanaknits Allhemp6, (100% hemp, 3½ oz./100g, 165 yd./151m) in Raspberry.

Kerchief

Using size 1 needles, CO 2 sts.

ROW 1 (RS): K all sts.

ROW 2: Inc 1, p.

ROW 3: Inc 1, k.

Rep Rows 2–3 once more—6 sts.

NEXT ROW: CO 1, p.

NEXT ROW: CO 1, k2 (including the CO st), *yo, SKP; rep from * to end of row.

Rep these 2 rows to desired size, changing to the circular needle when needed to accommodate the sts. (The scarf shown is worked until 173 sts.) BO very loosely.

Finishing

Fringe

Cut a length of cardboard 3½" (9cm) wide. Wrap yarn around numerous times. Cut along one edge. Using a size D/3 crochet hk insert the hk from back to front of Kerchief and pull the center of a fringe through about 1" (3cm). Bring the fringe ends through the loop and pull tight.

Weave in ends.

MORNING GLORY

A little zippered and hooded jacket to toss on and go, and made of soy to be warm like wool. The pattern stitch creates flattering diagonals, and the cut of the dolman sleeves reduces bulk at the underarms for a sleek fit.

SKILL LEVEL
Intermediate

METHOD
Knit and Crochet

SIZES
To fit actual bust/waist size: 31½/24 (34/26, 36/28, 39/31, 42/34)" (80/61 [86/66, 91/71, 99/79, 107/86]cm)

FINISHED MEASUREMENTS
Waist: Approx 28¾ (31¼, 33½, 37¼, 40¾)" (73 [79, 85, 95, 104]cm)

YARN
9 (9, 10, 10, 11) (3½ oz./100g, 175 yd./160m) skeins worsted weight yarn

NEEDLES
Size US 7 (4.5mm) straight needles

40" (100cm) size US 7 (4.5m) circular needle

40" (100cm) size US 8 (5mm) circular needle

1 extra US 7 (4.5mm) straight needle for three-needle bind off

If necessary, change needle size to obtain correct gauge.

HOOK
Size US F/5 (3.75mm) crochet hook

NOTIONS
Stitch markers

Yarn needle

Lightweight 14" (36cm) separating zipper to match yarn

Sewing needle

Thread to match yarn

GAUGE
20 sts and 28 rows = 4" (10cm) in patt st on size US 7 (4.5mm) needles

The project shown at right was made using South West Trading Company Phoenix (100% Soysilk, 3½ oz./100g, 175 yd./160m) in Sapphire.

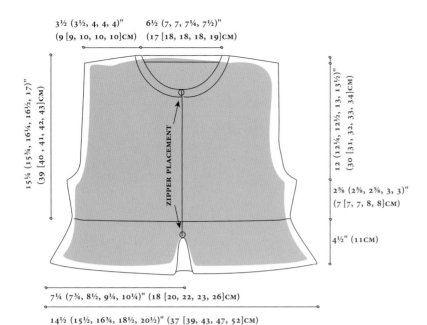

3½ (3½, 4, 4, 4)" 6½ (7, 7, 7¼, 7½)"
(9 [9, 10, 10, 10]CM) (17 [18, 18, 18, 19]CM)

ZIPPER PLACEMENT

15¾ (15¾, 16¼, 16½, 17)" (39 [40 , 41, 42, 43]CM)

12 (12¼, 12½, 13, 13½)" (30 [31, 32, 33, 34]CM)

2⅝ (2⅝, 2⅝, 3, 3)" (7 [7, 7, 8, 8]CM)

4½" (11CM)

7¼ (7¾, 8½, 9¼, 10¼)" (18 [20, 22, 23, 26]CM)

14½ (15½, 16¾, 18½, 20½)" (37 [39, 43, 47, 52]CM)

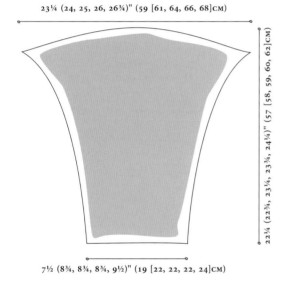

23¼ (24, 25, 26, 26¾)" (59 [61, 64, 66, 68]CM)

22¼ (22¾, 23¼, 23¾, 24¼)" (57 [58, 59, 60, 62]CM)

7½ (8¾, 8¾, 8¾, 9½)" (19 [22, 22, 22, 24]CM)

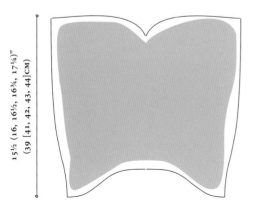

15½ (16, 16½, 16¾, 17¼)" (39 [41, 42, 43, 44]CM)

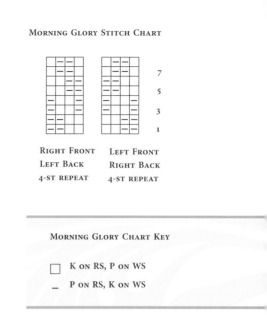

MORNING GLORY STITCH CHART

7
5
3
1

RIGHT FRONT   LEFT FRONT
LEFT BACK   RIGHT BACK
4-ST REPEAT   4-ST REPEAT

MORNING GLORY CHART KEY

☐ K ON RS, P ON WS

‒ P ON RS, K ON WS

PATTERN STITCH

2×2 RIB (MULT OF 4 STS)
ALL ROWS: [K2, p2] across.

Right Front

Note: This style is fitted to the waist. See the schematic for the length from shoulder to waist and, if needed, adjust the knitting to shorten or lengthen the area between the waist and the beg of the armhole.

Keep track of which side of the knitting you are working on by the location of the yarn tail. When the yarn tail is to the left, you are on the RS. When the yarn tail is to the right, you are on the WS.

Using size 7 needles, CO 36 (40, 44, 48, 52) sts. Beg Morning Glory Stitch Chart for Right Front, keeping in patt throughout.

At 1" (3cm), inc 1 st at the end of next RS row.

At 2" (5cm), inc 1 (1, 1 ,0, 1) sts at the end of next RS row—38 (42, 46, 49, 54) sts.

Armhole Shaping
When piece meas 2⅝ (2⅝, 2⅝, 3, 3)" (7 [7, 7, 8, 8]cm), BO 1 (1, 1, 2, 3) sts at beg of next WS row.

SIZE 42 ONLY: BO 2 sts at beg of next WS row. BO 1 st at beg of WS row every ½" (1cm) 5 times.

ALL SIZES: BO 1 st every 1" (3cm) at Armhole edge 4 (5, 6, 8, 3) times—33 (36, 39, 39, 41) sts. Work even in patt until piece meas 12 (12¼, 13, 13, 13⅜)" (30 [31, 33, 33, 34]cm).

Front Neck

BO 6 (7, 7, 6, 6) sts at beg of next RS row—27 (29, 32, 33, 35) sts.

BO 3 sts at beg of next RS row—24 (26, 29, 30, 32) sts.

BO 2 sts at beg of next RS row—22 (24, 27, 28, 30) sts.

SIZE 39 ONLY: BO 1 st at beg of next RS row—27 sts.

SIZE 42 ONLY: BO 2 sts at beg of next RS row—28 sts.

ALL SIZES: BO 1 st at beg of RS row 6 times—16 (18, 21, 21, 22) sts.

Shoulder Shaping

Work even until piece meas 14½ (15, 15¼, 15½, 16)" (37 [38, 39, 39, 41]cm), ending with a RS row.

BO 6 sts at beg of next WS row.

BO 6 sts at beg of next WS row.

BO 4 (4, 5, 6, 5) sts at beg of next WS row.

At beg of next WS row BO rem 0 (2, 4, 3, 4) sts.

Left Front

Foll Morning Glory Stitch Chart for Left Front, keeping in patt throughout. Foll shaping instructions for Right Front, reversing all shaping.

Back

CO 72 (80, 88, 96,104) sts, placing a marker at the center. With RS facing, beg Morning Glory Stitch patt, using chart for Right Back to the right of the marker, and the chart for Left Back to the left of the marker. Keep in patt throughout, slipping the marker on ea row.

At 1" (3cm), inc 1 (1, 1, 1, 1) st ea end of row.

At 2" (5cm) inc 1 (1, 1, 0, 1) sts at ea end of row—76 (84, 92, 98, 108) sts.

Work Armhole Shaping same as for Right Front, working the shaping at both edges at the same time—66 (72, 78, 78, 82) sts.

Back Neck

When piece meas 14 (14½, 14¾, 15, 15½)" (36 [37, 37, 38, 39]cm), on the RS, work 27 (28, 31, 30, 31) sts, join a second ball of yarn and BO center 12 (16, 16, 18, 18) sts, work to end.

At the same time, work Shoulder Shaping as for Right Front.

Working both sides of Back Neck at the same time,

BO 7 (6, 6, 6, 6) sts at Neck edge at beg of next 2 rows.

BO 3 (2, 2, 1, 2) sts at Neck edge at beg of next 2 rows.

BO 1 (1, 1, 1, 1) st at Neck edge at beg of next 2 rows.

BO 0 (1, 1, 1, 1) sts at Neck edge at beg of next 0 (2, 2, 2, 2) rows.

Peplum

Sew side seams. With RS facing and size 7 circular needle, pick up and k 1 st for ea st of Fronts and Back—144 (160, 176, 192, 208) sts. Work in St st.

ROW 1 (WS): P, dec 8 sts evenly across ea front section, and 16 sts across back.

Work even for 1" (3cm), on the final row place marker 20 sts before ea side seam, at ea side seam, and 20 sts after ea side seam (6 markers). Slip ea marker as you come to it.

NEXT ROW (RS): Change to size 8 needles and k to marker, inc, k1, inc, work up to next marker and rep incs as before. Work to end of row.

Note: Inc by picking up the horizontal thread between sts and k into the front of it.

Rep incs as est every 4th row.

When Peplum meas 3½" (9cm), end with a WS row.

Work in 2×2 Rib for 2 rows.

BO in patt.

Sleeves

CO 40 (44, 44, 48, 48) sts. Work in 2×2 Rib for 2 rows then change to St st. When piece meas 2" (5cm), inc 1 st ea side, and again at 3" (8cm)—44 (48, 48, 52, 52) sts.

Work even until piece meas 4" (10cm), ending with a WS row.

NEXT ROW (RS): Work first row of st patt. For Left Sleeve, use st patt for Right Front. For Right Sleeve, use st patt for Left Front. Stay in patt for rem of Sleeve. AT THE SAME TIME, beg shaping Sleeve.

Inc 1 st ea side of Sleeve every 4th row until there are 82 (86, 88, 92, 92) sts. Work even until piece meas 17⅜ (17⅜, 17¾, 18, 17⅛)" (44 [44, 45, 46, 43]cm), ending after a WS row.

FOR SIZES 31½ AND 34: Inc 1 st at beg of next 2 rows, then 3 sts at beg of next 8 rows, then 4 sts at beg of next 2 rows—116 (120) sts.

FOR SIZES 36 AND 39: Inc 1 st at beg of next 4 rows, then 3 sts at beg of next 8 rows, then 4 sts at beg of next 2 rows—124 (128) sts.

FOR SIZE 42: Inc 1 st at beg of next 4 rows, then inc 2 sts at beg of next 2 rows, then inc 3 sts at beg of next 8 rows, then inc 4 sts at beg of next 2 rows, then inc 5 sts at beg of next 2 rows—142 sts.

Sleeve Cap

FOR SIZE 42 ONLY: BO 2 sts at beg of next 4 rows, then 3 sts at beg of next 2 rows—128 sts. Cont as for all sizes.

BO 3 sts at beg of next 8 (10, 10, 10, 10) rows.

BO 4 sts at beg of next 4 rows.

BO 6 sts at beg of next 2 rows.

BO 12 sts at beg of next 2 rows.

BO rem 40 (38, 42, 46, 46) sts.

Hood

Using 2 balls of yarn CO 9 (11,12, 9, 12) sts from ea onto one needle.

Working in St st, k across one group of sts, then the other group, and p across both groups on the foll row.

NEXT ROW (RS): K across the first group of sts, then CO 3 sts at beg of 2nd group, work to end.

NEXT ROW (WS): P across first group, then CO 3 sts at beg of 2nd group—12 (14, 15, 12, 15) sts in ea section.

Cont in this manner, CO at the same edge and on every other row of ea section 3 sts 3 times—21 (23, 24, 21, 24) sts in ea section.

CO at same edge of ea section 2 sts twice—25 (27, 28, 25, 28) sts in ea section.

CO at same edge of ea section 4 sts on next 2 rows, then 5 sts on next 2 rows.

FOR SIZES 39 AND 42 ONLY: CO 3 sts at same edge of ea section—37 (40) sts. Piece should meas approx 3 (3, 3, 3⅛, 3⅛)" (8 [8, 8, 8, 8]cm).

CO 10 (9, 10, 10, 10) sts at center, joining the two sections on the foll row, and cut one ball of yarn—78 (81, 84, 84, 90) sts.

Work even until piece meas 13⅜ (13⅞, 14 ⅜, 14½, 15)" (34 [35, 36, 37, 38]cm).

NEXT ROW (RS): Work to center and BO 2 sts at center. Fasten on a second ball of yarn and work ea half of the Hood at the same time. At beg of ea row BO 2 sts on ea section twice, then 4 sts on ea section. BO rem 30 (32, 33, 33, 36) sts using three-needle BO.

Finishing

Weave in ends. Block ea piece. Sew Shoulder seams. Using size 7 needles and with RS facing, pick up and k 22 (24, 24, 25, 25) sts along Front Neck edge, 39 (40, 41, 41, 43) sts across Back Neck, and 22 (24 ,24, 25, 25) sts along rem Front edge. Work in St st for 1" (3cm) then BO all sts.

Sew Sleeves into Armholes, sew Sleeve and side seams. Sew rem seam of Hood, then sew Hood to Neck edge.

Using F/5 crochet hook and beg at bottom edge of a Front section, sc evenly up the Front opening edge, around the Hood and down the other Front. Fasten off.

Baste zipper inside the Front edges, placing it from the seam in which the Hood is fastened to the Neck edge, to and including the upper 1" (3cm) of the Peplum, so that the outer edge of the crochet meets the center of the zipper when closed. Fold the upper edges of excess zipper tape inwards. Use sewing thread and needle to hand sew in place using small sts along center of zipper tape, then loosely whipstitch the edges of the tapes to the sweater.

Cord (make 2, optional)

Using size F/5 crochet hook, make a chain 22 (24, 26, 28, 30)" (56 [61, 66, 71, 76]cm) long, turn and sl st along ch, working into both loops of ea ch, fasten off. Sew one to ea side of the zipper tape inside of the jacket. Carefully and evenly thread ea cord through sts at the top of the Peplum, bringing the ends out at the center back of the jacket. Draw up until the jacket fits closely, and tie the ends in a bow, tying a second time to knot.

Weave in remaining ends.

WAVES OF GRAIN

An easy four-row stitch pattern with two organic cotton yarns makes a rippled and striped scarf that is snuggly and soft to wear.

SKILL LEVEL
Beginner

METHOD
Knit

SIZE
One size

FINISHED MEASUREMENTS
Approx 7" × 43"
(18cm × 109cm)

YARN
1 (1¾ oz./50g, 92 yd./84m) skein worsted weight yarn (A)

1 (1¾ oz./50g, 135 yd./125m) skein worsted weight yarn (B)

NEEDLES
Size US 7 (4.5mm) straight needles

If necessary, change needle size to obtain correct gauge.

NOTIONS
Yarn needle

GAUGE
24 sts and 28 rows = 4" (10cm) in Wave Pattern

The project shown at right was made using Tahki Yarns Sky (100% biofil cotton, 1¾ oz./50g, 92 yd./84m) in color 1 (A) and Tahki Yarns Jeans (100% organic cotton, 1¾ oz./50g, 135 yd./125m) in color 001 (B).

PATTERN STITCH

WAVE PATTERN (MULT OF 3 STS)
ROW 1 (WS): K all sts.
ROW 2: K2, *yo, k4, [k2tog] twice, k4, yo, k1; rep from *, end with k1.
ROW 3: K2, p to last 2 sts, k2.
ROW 4: Rep Row 2.
Rep Rows 1–4 for patt.

Scarf
CO 42 sts. Work in Wave Pattern, changing colors as desired to form stripes, until Scarf is desired length or yarn is almost used up. End Scarf with Row 4. BO.

Finishing
Weave in ends. Lightly steam press.

A GIFT OF NETTLE

This bag is double-knitted as a hollow piece. Use it to give a small gift, or as a place to keep a piece of fine jewelry. A unique yarn will give great character to a finished piece. Decorate the bag as you like, or crochet Irish Roses and sew them on.

SKILL LEVEL
Beginner

METHOD
Knit and Crochet

SIZES
One size

FINISHED MEASUREMENTS
Approx 4½" × 5½" (11cm × 14cm)

YARN
1 (3 oz./90g, 200 yd./183m) skein sport weight yarn

NEEDLES
Size US 4 (3.5mm) straight needles

Set of 4 size US 4 (3.5mm) double pointed needles

HOOK
Size 2 (2.25mm) steel crochet hook

If necessary, change needle or hook size to obtain correct gauge.

NOTIONS
Stitch marker

Yarn needle

GAUGE
16 sts and 20 rows = 4" (10cm) in patt on size US 4 (3.5mm) needles

The project shown at right was made using Frabjous Fibers Nettle (100% nettle, 3 oz./90g, 200 yd./183m) in color Natural.

SLIP STITCH

ROW 1 (RS): [K1, bring yarn forward and sl next st pwise then bring yarn back] across.

ROW 2: K the sl sts from prev row, and sl the k sts. Work carefully, since any mistakes will keep the piece from opening up.

Rep Rows 1–2 for patt.

Bag

Using size 4 straight needles, CO 36 sts. Work in Slip Stitch until piece meas 4" (10cm). Separate the sts onto two dpns: sl the first st onto one dpn, and the next onto another. Cont until half of the sts are on one needle and half are on the another. The bag can now open. Divide the sts onto 3 dpns, place marker and beg working in the rnd.

Frilly Bag Top
Note: Inc by knitting into front then back of a st.

RND 1: [K2tog, yo] around.

RND 2 AND ALL EVEN ROWS: K all sts.

RND 3: [K1, inc in next st] around.

RNDS 5 AND 7: Inc in ea st around.

BO.

Finishing

Pull Cord
Using size 2 crochet hook, ch for 24" (61cm). Turn, then sl st in ea ch to end. Fasten off and weave in ends. Weave the cord through the yo's made in Rnd 1 of Frilly Bag Top.

Bag Bottom Edging
ROW 1: Using size 2 crochet hook, join yarn with a sl st onto one end of Bag Bottom, ch 1 and sc in same place. [Ch 3, sc into next "loop" of the knitted cast-on row] across, finishing with a sc. Turn.

ROW 2: [6 sc into loop, sl st into next sc] across. Fasten off.

To decorate the bag, crochet and sew on Irish Roses (see page 88) or the decor of your choice.

Weave in ends.

BASIC KNITTING INFORMATION

STANDARD KNITTING ABBREVIATIONS

approx	approximately
beg	beginning
BO	bind off
CC	contrast color
cn	cable needle
CO	cast on
cont	continue, continuing
dec	decrease
dpn(s)	double-pointed needle(s)
ea	each
est	establish, established
foll	following
inc	increase
k	knit
k2tog	knit 2 together
kwise	knitwise, as if to knit
MC	main color
mult	multiple
p	purl
(in) patt	(in pattern)
p2tog	purl 2 together
prev	previous
psso	pass slipped stitch over
pwise	purlwise
rem	remaining
rep	repeat
rnd	round
RS	right side
rep	repeat
SKP	slip 1, knit 1, pass slipped stitch over
sl	slip
st(s)	stitch(es)
St st	Stockinette stitch
tbl	through back loop
tog	together
WS	wrong side
w&t	wrap and turn
yo	yarn over

STANDARD U.S. CROCHET ABBREVIATIONS

ch	chain
dc	double crochet
dtr	double triple crochet
hdc	half double crochet
hk	hook
lp(s)	loop, loops
sc	single crochet
sp	space
tr	triple crochet

KNITTING NEEDLE CONVERSIONS

DIAMETER (MM)	U.S. SIZE
2	0
2.25	1
2.5	1½
2.75	2
3	2½
3.25	3
3.5	4
3.75	5
4	6
4.5	7
5	8
5.5	9
6	10
6.5	10½
8	11
9	13
10	15
12.75	17
15	19
20	36

HOOKS FOR YARN CROCHET

DIAMETER (MM)	U.S. SIZE
2.25	B/1
2.75	C/2
3.25	D/3
3.5	E/4
3.75	F/5
4	G/6
5	H/8
5.5	I/9
6	J/10
6.5	K/10½
8	L/11
9	M/13, N/13
10	N/15, P/15
15	p/Q
16	Q
19	S

HOOKS FOR THREAD CROCHET

DIAMETER (MM)	U.S. SIZE
.75	14
.85	13
1	12
1.1	11
1.3	10
1.4	9
1.5	8
1.65	7
1.8	6
1.9	5
2	4
2.1	3
2.25	2
2.75	1
3.25	0
3.5	00

YARN WEIGHT GUIDELINES

Since the names given to different weights of yarn can vary widely depending on the country of origin or the yarn manufacturer's preference, the Craft Yarn Council of America has put together a standard yarn weight system to impose a bit of order on the sometimes unruly yarn labels. Look for a picture of a skein of yarn with a number 0–6 on most kinds of yarn to figure out its "official" weight. Gauge is given over 4" (10cm) of Stockinette stitch. The information in the chart below is taken from www.yarnstandards.com.

	SUPER BULKY (6)	BULKY (5)	MEDIUM (4)	LIGHT (3)	FINE (2)	SUPERFINE (1)	LACE (0)
TYPE	bulky, roving	chunky, craft, rug	worsted, afghan, aran	dk, light, worsted	sport, baby	sock, fingering, baby	fingering, 10-count crochet thread
KNIT GAUGE RANGE	6–11 sts	12–15 sts	16–20 sts	21–24 sts	23–26 sts	27–32 sts	33–40 sts
RECOMMENDED NEEDLE IN U.S. SIZE RANGE	11 and larger	9 to 11	7 to 9	5 to 7	3 to 5	1 to 3	000 to 1

SUBSTITUTING YARNS

If you substitute yarn, be sure to select a yarn of the same weight as the yarn recommended for the project. Even after checking that the recommended gauge on the yarn you plan to substitute is the same as for the yarn listed in the pattern, make sure to knit a swatch to ensure that the yarn and needles you are using will produce the correct gauge.

RESOURCES

Plant-based yarns are easier to find every day and the following manufacturers offer some of my favorites. Contact them to find a retail source near you. Check out their Web sites to learn more about the yarns, browse available colors and find retail sources.

BERROCO, INC.
www.berroco.com

BLUE SKY ALPACAS, INC.
www.blueskyalpacas.com

CASCADE YARNS
www.cascadeyarns.com

THE DMC CORPORATION
www.dmc-usa.com

ECOBUTTERFLY
www.ecobutterfly.com

HALCYON YARN
www.halcyonyarn.com

HAND MAIDEN
www. handmaiden.ca

FRABJOUS FIBERS
www.frabjousfibers.com

HIMALAYA YARN
www.himalayayarn.com

KNIT ONE, CROCHET TOO, INC.
www.knitonecrochettoo.com

KNIT PICKS
www.knitpicks.com

KOLLAGE YARNS
www.kollageyarns.com

LACIS
www.lacis.com

LANAKNITS DESIGNS
www.lanaknits.com

LOUET NORTH AMERICA
www.louet.com

NORDIC MART
www.nordicmart.com

ROWAN YARNS
www.knitrowan.com
www.westminsterfibers.com

SOUTH WEST TRADING COMPANY
www.soysilk.com

TAHKI STACY CHARLES, INC.
www.tahkistacycharles.com

TANDY LEATHER FACTORY, INC.
www.tandyleatherfactory.com

WEBS
www.yarn.com

INDEX

FIND MORE GREAT PATTERNS IN THESE OTHER KNITTING BOOKS

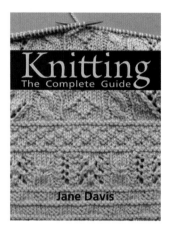

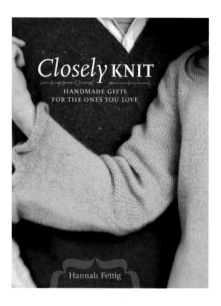

THE KNITCHICKS' GUIDE TO SWEATERS: CLASSIC STYLES FOR THE MODERN KNITTER

MARCELLE KARP AND PAULINE WALL

This book is a comprehensive and practical guide to knitting sweaters for women, children and men. The authors provide all the information you need to knit beautiful sweaters in a variety of styles. Additional tips and information from the authors can help you customize the sweaters, too!

ISBN-13: 978-1-60061-096-7
ISBN-10: 1-60061-096-X
PAPERBACK • 144 PAGES • Z2005

KNITTING THE COMPLETE GUIDE

JANE DAVIS

Knitting The Complete Guide is a resource knitters can rely on for years to come. With a collection of 200 pattern stitches and a lay-flat format, this book is a quick and easy guide to all things knitting.

ISBN-13: 978-0-89689-591-1
ISBN-10: 0-89689-591-2
HARDCOVER WITH CONCEALED
SPIRAL • 256 PAGES • Z1480

CLOSELY KNIT: HANDMADE GIFTS FOR THE ONES YOU LOVE

HANNAH FETTIG

Closely Knit is filled with thoughtful knitted gifts to fit all the people you love. From luxurious scarves and wearable sweaters to cozy socks, there is something for everyone on your list. Each project is rated with a handy time guide so you can choose what to knit based on how much time you have.

ISBN-13: 978-1-60061-018-9
ISBN-10: 1-60061-018-8
PAPERBACK • 144 PAGES • Z1280

Discover imagination, innovation and inspiration at **www.mycraftivity.com**. Connect. Create. Explore.